TENDULKAR
10

SACHIN
Genius Unplugged

SACHIN
Genius Unplugged

Westland Ltd
Venkat Towers , 165, P.H. Road, Maduravoyal , Chennai 600095
No.38/10 (New No.5), Raghava Nagar , New Timber Yard Layout, Bangalore 560026
Survey No. A-9, II Floor, Moula Ali Industrial Area , Moula Ali, Hyderabad 500040
23/181, Anand Nagar, Nehru Road, Santacruz East, Mumbai 400055
47, Brij Mohan Road, Daryaganj, New Delhi 110002

First published in India by Westland Ltd in association with KRAB Media & Marketing, 2011

KRAB Media & Marketing
Email: info@krabmedia.com
www.krabmedia.com

10 9 8 7 6 5 4 3 2

ISBN: 978-93-80658-17-9

Printed at Manipal Press Limited, Manipal

SACHIN
Genius Unplugged

Edited by
Suresh Menon

Published by

westland

in association with

krab
WWW.KRABMEDIA.COM

SAHARA

INSIDE

Dilmah
SRI LANKA
CBFS
CBFS
CBFS

FOREWORD

Muttiah Muralitharan

I never shared a dressing room with Sachin Tendulkar, and in some twenty years of international cricket that was my one regret. We have always been in opposition, whether it was a charity match or an international, so I know all about Sachin's inside-out cover drive or his quicksilver footwork, but precious little about how he reacted to poor decisions or poor scores. There is nothing like sharing a dressing room to really understand a player away from his public image, and closer to the heart of who he really is.

Yet, I know instinctively that there is no great difference between the public Sachin and the man he is in private. The instinct is endorsed by stories I hear from his colleagues. Sachin is a man of great dignity, and those of us who played together in the same era must consider ourselves lucky. It is remarkable that a man can play for so long as he has at the international level, and not only create records that seem unapproachable, but play through without a single black mark against his name. That is what makes him truly great.

I first met him during the Hero Cup tournament in India in 1993. We had all heard about him, of course. Of how he had made his debut in Pakistan as a 16-year-old, and how after a tour of Australia at 19 he was already being spoken of as the best batsman in the world. He batted five or six overs in that game in Kanpur, and remained unbeaten in his twenties as India won, but that was enough. You don't need to hear a whole song to know its greatness; nor eat a whole dish to know it is a gastronomic delight.

The Sachin sampler was enough. All the stories we had heard were true. The more forward-looking of our bowlers realised that he was bound to be a terror, a thorn in our side for years and years to come. Some of us looked forward to the challenge of denying him the joy of putting us to the sword. I remember thinking to myself, 'this boy is going to be one of the greatest ever in the game.' I wasn't too far from being known as a 'boy' myself, but I was a year older than Sachin and reserved the right to call him 'boy'!

Our first Test match together was in my home town of Kandy, but it was washed out; I didn't play the next Test, where Sachin got a century, and when I returned for the third Test, he made 71.

Two things stood out as he continued to dominate. He had the remarkable ability to hit the ball exactly where he wanted to, as if his natural ball sense was aligned to eyes that scanned the field at 360 degrees. He simply murdered the loose delivery, invariably hitting a boundary off it, even in the midst of a defensive spell of batting. It meant he scored at a rate that was discouraging to the bowlers.

I have often been asked what my strategy against him was. I focussed on not bowling a loose delivery; it gave you some chance on your good day! Yet he was perfectly capable of sending your best deliveries to the boundary too, and must have broken the hearts of more bowlers than any other batsman.

In the 90s and even later, the comparison was always with Brian Lara, the other great batsman of the period. Sachin was more consistent, a run machine. These two batsmen are the best I have bowled to.

Over the years, Sachin the batsman changed a lot. His all-out aggression in the early years was replaced by a more mature, less risk-taking attitude. But the runs continued to flow till at the age of 37 he showed how he could be both aggressive and safe by making one-day cricket's first double hundred and following that with a double hundred in a Test against Australia.

Sachin has pushed the limits of the possible, and I can't imagine anyone breaking his records – not for the next 100 years anyway!

Through it all, Sachin has remained a private individual, almost shy (but very talkative and fun-loving in a close group of friends), and I have always respected that. When your fans call you 'God' it is difficult not to believe it yourself, but Sachin is one of the most grounded people I know.

The only disappointing aspect of his cricket has been his captaincy; I sympathised a lot with him because one man cannot do every job, but he had the self-knowledge to give up the post and focus on contributing to victories with his bat. And that's what matters in the final analysis.

Sachin is a great hero in Sri Lanka as he is wherever cricket is played, and youngsters want to emulate him. He brings together in him all that is best in the game, and for that reason he is for me the face of the game.

I am confident that this book of essays edited by Suresh Menon will throw light on the various aspects of this genius from Mumbai whose constituency extends over the entire cricket-playing world.

Coca-Cola
Coca-Cola
Coca-Cola

INTRODUCTION

Shakespeare was wrong. It is not the good that is oft interred with the bones, as he makes Mark Anthony say. It is the humanness of the human being – the foibles, the growing pains, the less-than-perfect days that are forgotten when legends grow.

Sometimes the legacy of great players is restricted to one or two major achievements, sometimes the legend grows in the opposite direction with each passing year following retirement. Already Kapil Dev, for example, is simply the man who led India to a World Cup. He was much more, and his impact was far greater, but it is convenient to hang '1983' around his neck and leave it at that. The legend of the great Indian spinners has only grown, although the last of Bedi, Prasanna, Chandrasekhar, Venkatraghavan, quit international cricket nearly three decades ago.

Like writers and artists, sportsmen are subject to revisionism, with fresh assessments adding to the known portrait.

A good place to start is the contemporary report. How was a player received in his own time? Sometimes reputations grow with every ball not bowled or every stroke not played, but it is always fascinating to know what writers think without the benefit of hindsight.

These essays on Sachin Tendulkar are by writers who have been reporting his game, analysing his batting, placing him in context, criticising him, praising him over the years. It is a first draft of biography.

Not surprisingly, everyone has a personal Sachin story as well as a measured professional story, and part of the joy of the book is to read the admission by veteran writers like Mike Coward on how the player figures in his bank accounts, for example. Harsha Bhogle's first interview with the teenager Sachin, Osman Samiuddin's discussion with his mathematician father, Barney Ronay's air-cricket in the Tendulkar manner, and personal insights by Rahul Dravid, Anil Kumble, Bishan Bedi throw light on Tendulkar, on the writers, and on the art of sportswriting itself.

It was the former India captain Dilip Vengsarkar who first spoke to me about Tendulkar. "He is a combination of Sunil Gavaskar and Gundappa Vishwanath," he said. This was a startling way to describe a 15-year-old, placing him on a pedestal above both India's greatest defensive batsman and her most creative run-getter.

Sachin goes past Sunil Gavaskar with his 35th Test century.

Within a couple of years, Tendulkar showed this was no exaggeration. His first century, a match-saving effort at Old Trafford was in the Gavaskar mould. The next two, in Sydney and Perth, would have made Vishwanath proud. And he hadn't turned 19 yet.

In 1989, Tendulkar made his international debut in Pakistan. Of his teammates then, one has become an insufferable television commentator, and two others have become decent ones; one has been convicted of murder, and another banned for life for match-fixing. One eliminated the line between whistle-blower and perpetrator; one has turned his energies to golf, two became chairmen of selectors. Two were elected Members of Parliament. One has dropped out of the public eye and another has turned television actor.

The idea for this book grew out of a casual long-distance conversation with a former colleague and friend, M Satyanarayan. His enthusiasm and energy were the initial driving force, and my thanks to him. The Abu Dhabi-based Satya teamed up with Diinesh Kumble of KRAB Media and Marketing who gave breath to the concept. Without Diinesh Kumble's guidance and sheer professionalism, this project would not have matured. I owe him profound thanks.

Now only one thing remained – to bring the superstars of the written word under one roof, as it were.

My thanks to the writers, friends all, and favourite reads over the years, who responded with enthusiasm: Mike Marqusee, Peter Roebuck, Greg Baum, Ayaz Memon, R Mohan, Gideon Haigh, Makarand Waingankar, Harsha Bhogle, Osman Samiuddin, Mike Coward, Barney Ronay. Thanks to Bishan Bedi, Anil Kumble, Rahul Dravid and Sanjay Manjrekar for their unique insights, and to Muttiah Muralitharan for the foreword.

Thanks to Ananthanarayanan who provided the statistics, to Diinesh Kumble, Anil Kumble, Pradeep Mandhani, Getty Images, Poorna Chander, Gulf News for the photographs, and to Tushar Menon for reading an early version and making suggestions.

And finally, thanks to Sachin Tendulkar himself, for providing joy to so many, employment to many, and to borrow from Roebuck, for giving us the privilege of writing on the game when he is its leading exponent.

S.M.

FOCUS, FOCUS, FOCUS

Harsha Bhogle

There has always been drama around him but not in his mind

Even as a child, Sachin Tendulkar built monuments; giant structures that forced you to transfer your gaze and then lock it on him. At fourteen, when good cricketers would be happy to come home with a half century, and get an appreciative pat from indulgent parents, he had a partnership of 664 and in five innings had made 1028 runs.

By fourteen, he had created expectations and had already started matching them. It was to set the pattern for an astonishing career. The monuments kept coming, the expectations grew frightening. It is not easy going to bed aware that success is a mere par score. It is a trait that defines champions and it defined even a fourteen year old.

Few people in Mumbai had seen him then but an extraordinarily large number knew of him. And it was around then, as an advertising executive hoping to get a by-line, that a simple brief arrived my way. Mudar Patherya, himself a young man and part of a young magazine called *Sportsworld*, wanted an article on the greatest schoolboy cricketer ever. It had to be typed on a manual typewriter and sent by post.

I was to discover then that, even at such a tender age, Sachin was already protected; insulated from distractions. He was to say many years later that anything that was likely to divert his mind was prohibited by an extraordinarily generous older brother. It was to sow the seeds for his legendary focus on the game. And so I had to call his brother who gave me an appointment and asked that I meet him first. I found it incredible, this was only a child I was going to meet, but I played along, part curious, part in admiration.

Twenty three years later Sanjay Manjrekar told me of how Sachin never allowed his mind to wander from the game, from the job at hand, from the activity that he was so passionate about. There has always been drama around him but not in his mind. It is there that he finds the calmness so necessary to perform; indeed so necessary to live up to the unreal expectations we have of him. I asked him what he was thinking about when he went out to bat. And he said "nothing". The mind

How to focus: two geniuses compare notes. With Shane Warne

has already been programmed for instinct to take over. It is something that even great shooters will tell you; that the mind must be free of thought. Don't try it for as a Buddhist monk once told me on a travel show I was doing "The mind is like a monkey, forever jumping around. Only through meditation can you learn to focus on one thing at a time."

I am sure there are things he doesn't like but they will not enter the world of Sachin the batsman. Maybe, just maybe, they had to enter the world of Sachin the captain because that was inhabited by a wider, more heterogenous set of people with different values. I just wonder if that was why he struggled as captain. In his world, he set his rules and followed them. Not everyone could do that and so, maybe, his mind wasn't as free of distraction as normal.

It is my deep belief though that eventually it is the person within who defines the sportsman the world sees. Sachin gives the world the impression that he always places the game above him, above the individual. But he is able to do so consistently because that is the way he is. He still thinks he is indebted to the game whereas an astonishingly large army of followers believe he has enriched it; that he almost owns it. And that is why he is able to approach situations with such equanimity.

He still thinks he is indebted to the game

I remember a moment in England, might have been at Lord's, where he was walking back to the pavilion and an idiot jumped the fences and walked alongside him, dancing around like a buffoon. Throughout the thirty yards Sachin walked as if he didn't know there was anyone else near him. He didn't abuse him, didn't bring him down with a tackle, didn't complain, just walked serenely on.

Sachin is at his best, feeling good and playing well, when he is fully fit. When he carries a niggle or an injury, he knows he has to allow for it. He will then adapt and still find shots to play within this unwelcome limitation imposed on him. In the final of IPL 3, it was apparent that he would be in a lot of pain but that is something that professional sportsmen have to live with. A tear in the webbing meant that he wouldn't have the power behind the shots. And yet he almost took his franchise home. As indeed he did in that wonderful Test match at Chennai in 1999, when the crowds put sport ahead of petty jingoism and congratulated Pakistan on a dramatic win. Aware that his back wouldn't support him all the way he launched into a flurry of shots to try and collect as many as he could. It was almost enough; it would have been if the last four had scored four each!

In his second coming in 2009-10, I asked him if anything had changed. "Yes," he said with a child like glee. "I'm completely fit." It was as if the carburettor had been cleansed of its last trace of impurity and the engine could now purr on as its master desired. The period before had probably been his worst as one injury after another laid into him and a nation was introduced to

Sachin celebrates in typical fashion after a double century against Australia in Bangalore.

different parts of the human anatomy! "I'm sick of this rehab" he confessed in 2008 and it struck me then that it would be an injury rather than a bowler that would eventually finish his career.

But he kept at it with resilience and discipline, two defining possessions of his that have been shrouded, and consequently undervalued, by his genius. Midway through 2010 he announced that he was looking forward to the next eighteen months, a period that would take him through to 38 and a staggering twenty two years at the highest level. But at the root of that desire was the confidence that his body would hold for he had trained like he had never trained before. Many of his younger team-mates see this resilience and discipline but find it too rigorous to embrace.

He didn't take to T20 very easily when it first came along. You would have thought that his naturally attacking style would be tailor-made for a batting-friendly format. But it took him time to come to terms with the fact that the risk behind a shot could be weighted in favour of getting out. Like all great players he valued his wicket greatly; it had to be earned and it could not be acquired through an unnecessarily rash shot. Accordingly his first instinct was to bat through the innings and let the strokeplayers play around him. But like with everything else in life he came around and devised a way like only he can.

And during IPL 3 he showed the world another way to play the game; not full of mindless slogs and contorted scoops but with classical strokeplay. Till the final, when he was way ahead of everyone else in terms of runs scored, he had hit but one six. Just one in fourteen T20 games! He had retained the elegance and correctness of his strokeplay and in doing so showed that if you hit the gaps consistently you don't have to hit it to the spectator!

Many years ago, two decades ago as I type this, he played against an England side that had Eddie Hemmings in it. Hemmings had made his first class debut seven years before Sachin was born. Now having gone past the stage of playing alongside, and against, players who were in their nappies while he batted against Wasim Akram, he is now playing in a new era; of players born in the post Sachin generation! It is time to say that good wine must age like him; mellow and smooth but still capable of producing a wondrous sigh.

People often wonder what he will do once he is done with playing with the game. The media as a career will not challenge him enough, certainly not the way it is evolving in India. He won't make a great coach simply because he will see the game in a light that his wards may not always be able to comprehend; his solutions, like mathematical proofs, might be beyond common reach. When he finds talent not walking step by step with work ethic, it will frustrate him. But eventually he will come to terms with waking up to something other than a cricket match. The question though is: will India?

HARSHA BHOGLE is one of the world's best-known television commentators. He was voted 'favourite cricket commentator' by Cricinfo readers in a poll in 2008.

THE SECULAR SAINT

Greg Baum

Outside the laws or outside the off stump, he could not be lured

The two keenest appreciations of Sachin Tendulkar were made from vantage points that could not have been more opposite to each other, and together serve as an incontrovertible cross-reference to his greatness. The first was Sir Donald Bradman's famous remark to his wife during the 1996 World Cup that Tendulkar put him in mind of how he himself batted.

The second is the widespread understanding in the cricket community that match-fixers will not successfully get on with their crooked business until Tendulkar is out, and an anecdotal account of how Tendulkar once unwittingly ruined a fix by batting too blissfully well.

It must be understood that neither reflection would have been made lightly. Sir Donald was not given to hyperbole or glibness, but rather was precise in everything he did and said. Nor would the fixers have bothered with throwaway lines.

Together, these tributes convey immutable impressions of Tendulkar that accord with less quantifiable, more aesthetic understandings of the glory of his batsmanship. Here is a man capable of changing the course of any game. Here is a man incorruptible in the face of the venal temptations that so many of his peers could not resist. Outside the laws or outside the off stump, he could not be lured. Here is a man not susceptible to human failing in any endeavour, a man not so much invincible as invulnerable.

Here is a man whose name is synonymous with purity, of technique, philosophy and image. If Ian Botham can be seen as the Errol Flynn of cricket, or Viv Richards as the Martin Luther King, or Shane Warne as the Marilyn Monroe, or Muttiah Muralitharan as the hobbit, Tendulkar is surely the game's secular saint.

Right from the beginning, he appeared to be touched by divinity. He came among us as a boy-god, unannounced. He was 16 and was hit on the head in his first appearance, but neither flinched nor retreated a step. Nothing thenceforth could harm him, temporal or otherwise. He was short and stocky - like all the best - and mop-topped and guileless to behold. He has scarcely changed since.

Watching the ball from the bowler's hand to the wicket keeper's.

Tendulkar was born with extravagant natural talent, but he was also driven and indefatigable. When a boy, he would bat from dawn to dusk, and even a little beyond. As with all the greats, he came not from another dimension, nor the mystical east, but from the nets. By such dedication, he came to understand intimately his own gift, and at length to lavish it upon others.

He came not from another dimension
but from the nets

His movements at the crease are small but exact. He said once that he did not believe in footwork for its conventional purpose, because the tempo of Test cricket did not permit a batsman the textbook indulgence of getting to the pitch of the ball. Rather, he thought of footwork as a means of balancing himself up at the crease so that each shot was hit just as he meant it. He scores predominantly through the off side, an unusual characteristic for such a heavy run-maker, but of course he can play every shot.

Tendulkar's method promotes an air of calm, reassurance and poise at the crease. Brian Lara's batting is characterised by explosion and violence, and Steve Waugh's by grim resolve, but Tendulkar's ways are timeless. His battles with Shane Warne, genius versus genius, have been for the ages. It is said that the common element to concepts of beauty among all peoples is symmetry, a balance between all the parts. So it is with Tendulkar's batting.

How easily he carries the hopes and takes responsibility for the wellbeing of untold millions on that impossible subcontinent; in this, he is also divine. All eyes are upon him, day and night, but no scandal has attached itself, not in his private life nor in his cricket endeavours. Across the land, he is the little man on the big posters and hoardings, creating a kind of reverse Big Brother effect; he is not watching them, but they are watching him. Still he stands tall.

Sometimes petty criticism is made that he fails India in its hours of need, but it is not borne out by the figures, and besides, no one man could take upon his shoulders all of India's needy hours.

When called upon, he also bowls intelligently, if sparingly. He is sure in the field. There is even about him, as there was about many saints, something of the ingenue. He is not a natural captain for the modern era because he can lead only by example. He does not have a charismatic presence in a cricket stadium, but rather fills it in a different way, as the one certainty in a sea of doubt. Batting is the most fraught of sporting pursuits because even for the best the end is only ever one ball away. Tendulkar seems to turn that verity upon itself.

As Tendulkar put Bradman in mind of himself, so he puts others in mind of Bradman. Once I was on a night train winding down from Simla to Kalka that stopped halfway for refreshments at a station lit by flaming torches. On a small television screen wreathed in cigarette smoke in the corner of the dining room Tendulkar was batting in a match in Mumbai. No one moved or spoke or looked away. The train was delayed by 20 minutes. Not until Tendulkar was out could the world resume its normal timetables and rhythms.

GREG BAUM is the Chief Sportswriter of The Age in Melbourne.

adidas
Airtel
Airtel
Airtel
Airtel
Airtel
Airtel
Airtel
Airtel
Airtel
Airtel
Airtel
Airtel
Airtel
Airtel
Airtel

THE ONE CONSTANT

Ayaz Memon

Batting is of course about making runs, but even more about knowing how to make runs

The Muse of History, condemned to brevity, might term Sachin Tendulkar as "one of the greatest cricketers of all time." That, however, would be stating the obvious - and alas, saying all too little.

So voluminous have been his achievements, so mighty their impact on the game (and perhaps more significantly, his country), that it would require several tomes to do justice to these. To write a mere essay on Tendulkar is like trying to climb Everest in a day. To borrow from Churchill, it is an assignment that is 'hopeless, but not impossible.'

Tendulkar made his Test debut, as everyone knows, on November 15, 1989 at Karachi against Pakistan; a callow 16-year-old with a mop of fuzzy hair, a squeaky voice and a world record already under his belt. Those with a penchant for seeing things through the prism of history might remember that this happened less than a week after the collapse of the Berlin Wall and less than three weeks before V P Singh was chosen Prime Minister of India to break the hegemony of the Congress and usher in the era of coalition politics.

The bald fact is that he has been around for 21 years. In almost every which way, the world has changed for India and Indians since then, except for one constant: the sight of a 5 foot 5 inch batsman walking out with his inordinately heavy bat, doing duty for the country, carrying the burden of expectations of a billion people, and more often than not fulfilling it.

But the magnitude of Tendulkar's achievement is not in mere longevity of tenure, though that is not insignificant either. Twenty years is a couple of lifetimes in any discipline. Only a handful from any discipline has had the physical wherewithal - and more importantly the motivation and mental toughness - to go through the rigours of professional sport year after year without flagging.

Hands, feet, eyes - everything in alignment as Sachin follows the ball.

Barely a dozen players in the history of cricket have played that long – but nobody has spent as many days on the field playing for his country. And with such remarkable consistency and virtuosity in run-scoring that the oft-abused definition 'genius' finds credence.

Tendulkar entered my life when I was in serious debate with myself about continuing writing on cricket. In my 'debut' series in 1982-83, I had seen Imran Khan devastate India with 40 wickets. A few months later, I saw Kapil Dev hold aloft the Prudential World Cup on the Lord's balcony. Three years later, I watched Javed Miandad hit the last ball six in Sharjah which was to stupefy Indians, cricketers and others, for almost a decade.

The following year, I saw Gavaskar complete 10,000 Test runs and then play his swansong – a technically brilliant but futile 96 against Pakistan at Bangalore. The next season, I saw Viv Richards make a masterly century at Delhi to reaffirm just why he was the best batsman of his time. By this time, I was becoming weary of cricket writing and travel. A sense of pervasive déjà vu seemed to have set in: been there, done that, is there anything more to see?

He must rate among the top ten batsmen of all time in terms of technical certitude, style and consistency

There was. The first clear evidence I had of Tendulkar's intrinsic and exceptional cricketing brilliance was almost 18 months before he made his entry at the international level when I went to see him bat in a schools match at the Cricket Club of India in early 1988. He had by then already announced his arrival to the world with the 664-runs partnership with schoolmate Vinod Kambli that found them a hallowed spot in *Wisden Cricketers' Almanack.*

But journalists are skeptics by nature, and I was seeking further vindication of his talent. The under-15 age group competitions, in any case, can be terribly misleading and abound with flukes and premature burn-outs. There had been several 'boy wonders' in Indian cricket, but few who had gone on to live up to their promise.

I was to join the then India captain Dilip Vengsarkar at the CCI for the match. Indeed, he goaded me into going there. "This boy Sachin is approaching another hundred," he called to say. By the time I reached the ground, however, Tendulkar was already past the three figure mark, and was now striking the ball with such gusto that the opposing fielders were left panting and virtually waving their hands in surrender.

But the match obviously had to continue, and in the hope of stemming the flow of runs, or of the batsman holing out, the fielding captain pushed his fielders deep. Tendulkar, however, was not to be suckered and changed his tactics: from hitting lusty boundaries, he began pushing for singles and twos. Then, when the fielding captain brought the field in again, he started hitting over the top again.

SAHARA

"The boy is destined for greatness," quipped the late Raj Singh Dungarpur, then president of the CCI and Indian cricket's eternal romantic, who was also witness to the proceedings from the pavilion. "Batting is of course about making runs, but even more about knowing how to make runs."

My favourite Tendulkar story, however, comes from another early encounter, some months after watching him dazzle at the CCI and earn encomiums from Vengsarkar and Raj Singh. By then he had made a hundred on debut in the Ranji Trophy, in the Duleep Trophy and the Irani Trophy. Tendulkar, not quite 16, had pitchforked himself into national reckoning. He was on everybody's short list for the tour of the West Indies in early 1989, but when the team was announced, his name was missing.

On the eve of the team's departure for the Caribbeans, the actor Tom Alter and I were to interview Dilip Vengsarkar for a sports video and thought it would be a good idea to include a section with the young cricketer too. Tendulkar was visibly chagrined at his omission in spite of his prolific run-getting in the domestic tournaments.

"The selectors wanted to protect you from Malcolm Marshall and Courtney Walsh," Tom and I told him. This appeared to rile him even further. "I'm not afraid of pace," he shot back, bristling with barely concealed unhappiness. "If I am hit, I will only learn faster." Tom's eyes popped out at the lad's self-assurance; I could only marvel in silence.

Everybody knows how he picked himself up after getting his nose bloodied by a snorter from Waqar Younis at Sialkot in the final Test of his first series and hit the next ball through covers for a boundary. In a flash, the self-effacing boy had become a man, inured to the pains and travails of international sport, instead relishing every minute of the challenge that this presented him. A star had been born.

Over the next few years, Tendulkar was to be identified the world over as a cricketer who belonged to the 'rarest of rare' categories; thereafter his intrinsic talent, the willingness to learn, the deep desire to succeed and an indomitable spirit were to repeat themselves several times to establish his greatness without dispute.

In the 20-odd years since his debut, I have rarely seen Tendulkar relax in the middle, or take his success for granted. Has he been the greatest batsman of all time? Arguably not, for, to get past Sir Don Bradman, the only sportsperson whose one statistic spells peerless achievement, seems an almost impossible task. If any other player finishes with a career Test average of even 75, leave aside 99.94, the comparison is plausible, not otherwise.

Has Tendulkar been the best batsman of his generation? More likely, though Brian Lara and Ricky Ponting will have so many votaries of their own that no clear conclusion is possible even here. Has he been better than Grace, Ranji, Trumper, Hobbs, Hammond, Hutton, the three Ws, Kanhai, Gavaskar, Border, Miandad, Greg Chappell - to name a few - who have illuminated the spectrum of batsmanship through the past 130 years and more? There will be pros and cons in reasonable quantities in this debate too.

Sir Don Bradman meets the man he said was his successor.

The two Little Masters: Sachin with Sunil Gavaskar.

I would venture, though, that he must rate amongst the top ten batsmen of all time in terms of technical certitude, style and consistency. He has scored the most runs in Tests and One-day internationals, as also most centuries in both these forms. In themselves, these are enough reasons to establish a giant who would straddle across the game's history with his greatness unquestioned in any era. The only bleak part would be his captaincy stint, which was nondescript.

But to measure Tendulkar's impact only through runs and centuries is limiting in its understanding of the phenomena in the Indian context. What he has done for Indian cricket with his remarkable batsmanship is more easily understood than the indelible impact he has had on the Indian psyche for the past twenty years. To explain this, I can do no better than to quote from a birthday tribute I wrote in 2008:

"Like cinema and politics, cricket is wholly integrated into Indian life. Tendulkar not only filled up stadiums around the country with his dynamic batsmanship, but also filled the nation with hope. At the physical level, he was playing sport, at a subliminal level he was nurturing the ambitions of a young country that was breaking its shackles from a restrictive past.

"The boy is destined for greatness," quipped the late Raj Singh Dungarpur, Indian cricket's eternal romantic

"For those in the know of Indian politics, Tendulkar had arrived when the Mandal agitation on the issue of reservations for scheduled and backward castes was at its peak. He was quickly to demonstrate that where skill was concerned, reservation was unwanted, merit is what should matter. So great was his talent and such was his appeal that he was to become the country's most recognised face within months of his playing international cricket.

"Willy-nilly, he was also to become the symbol of economic liberalisation too when he became the country's highest earning sportsperson through endorsements and the like. The equation between performance and reward was never clearer, and there could not have been a more deserving person either."

I dare say, that if Tendulkar were not around, the match-fixing controversy would have debilitated the game in the Indian sub-continent. The credibility vested in Tendulkar (and by extension, in players like Sourav Ganguly, Rahul Dravid and Anil Kumble) helped Indian cricket emerge from that crisis relatively unaffected. People trusted him, and belief in Indian cricket returned soon.

Equally remarkably, for all his phenomenal fame, all the glory and the wealth that has come his way, Tendulkar retains his humility and childlike enthusiasm for the game still. He is shy and introverted, a man of many strokes but few words, preferring to let his bat do the talking. When he does speak or take a position, however, the world listens, as happened in the Harbhajan Singh controversy in Australia in 2008.

Tendulkar has frequently been compared to Don Bradman as a batsman. This has its genesis in Bradman himself revealing in the 90s that he saw shades of himself in Tendulkar's batting, more specifically the on drive and the short arm pull. But for me the greater similarity is in the influence they have wielded, on the game in their countries; in the manner in which both have coped with the phenomenal pressures of personal and public expectation and lived up to it.

No two wickets in the history of the game have been as coveted by opposing teams as theirs; no two wickets in the history of the game meant so much for so many people for so long. Through their cricketing excellence, Bradman and Tendulkar not only established the identity of their respective nations on the world but, in the process, helped millions of their countrymen find their national identity too. For all his centuries and records that, to me, is the true essence of Tendulkar.

If that still doesn't resolve the issue of who's been the greatest batsman of all time, let me approach it differently. If Tendulkar were to retire tomorrow, a long queue of the game's greatest batsmen would await him near the dressing room: Hammond, Hobbs, Hutton, the three Ws, Richards, Gavaskar, Dravid, Sehwag, Ponting, Lara, Chappell, Miandad, et al. And at the head of this queue would be Bradman, first to shake his hand and say, "Well played you little bonzer!"

AYAZ MEMON, author and television personality has been writing on the game for three decades.

adidas
Airtel

PEPSI
MRF

BORDER ISSUES

Osman Samiuddin

Multan was about the adjustment of a star to the galaxy around him

In recalling a Sachin Tendulkar moment, it must be acknowledged that there is no small, hidden gem somewhere that others are unlikely to have seen, like the single of a cherished band recorded during lost days available only in B-side bootlegs. His great innings, his great failures, his shots: put together, everyone remembers everything about him. There is no exclusivity in the Tendulkar experience. This is no crib, merely proof that true greatness seeps through all over the universe.

Still, there is a three-ball mini epic. It came in 2003, at Centurion which is not as intimidating a venue as the name suggests, in a World Cup game against Pakistan. It was built on the battle with Shoaib Akhtar, in a way bigger than the game itself. A rabid machismo and jingoism was polluting the air; Shoaib was strutting, Virender Sehwag was too but with greater discretion. Waqar, Wasim were around, Ganguly was captain; you could smell it off the TV in lounges everywhere.

First came the six, reaching and tipped over deep point as if he were helping a speedy ball along to its inevitable destination. Immediately it went into folklore. This part was mano-a-mano, man on man: who has the biggest? Second came the flick through square leg, which is not so much a shot as it is the autograph on all his innings. This part was Sachin against Shoaib, wristy Indian batting taking on full length Pakistani fast bowling, tradition clashing with tradition.

Authority built, now dominance had to be shown. It came with the third part, the most magnificent and the one Tendulkar shot which I cannot forget. It was a good ball, on a length, outside off and quick. Tendulkar's response looked appropriate; a discreet shuffle into line, straight bat down in defense, bat swing dead on contact with ball, good defence. Except, as the ball gathered pace past the stumps and much to the left of mid-on, and gradually to tease mid-on all the way to the boundary, it revealed itself to be, astoundingly, a stroke of attack. Man on man, tradition against tradition and now, with finality, genius against mortal; nothing more was to come from that match for Pakistan.

◄ *Wasim Akram makes his feelings known as Sachin enjoys the moment.*

Over the previous week I had been having a discussion with my father. He is a retired professor of statistics and around that time had begun to get into the game, having avoided it through much of his life. We were comparing Tendulkar and Rahul Dravid. My father, logician and statistician, argued that instead of calculating batting averages, we should calculate standard deviations, which are essentially a more accurate gauge of consistency; a measure of how far a batsman, each time he goes to the crease, will deviate from his average. Dravid you will find, my father said, will have a lower SD, proof thus that he is a more consistent batsman which within the world of statistics is gold and must necessarily mean that he is the better.

'Mein khelega' he said after a bouncer nearly broke his nose on debut. So he did, unlike anyone

My father is not an inflexible man though, so having seen that shot – and then the rest of that innings - he acknowledged that yes, perhaps Dravid cannot do that.

The first time I saw Tendulkar bat live in a Test was in an empty, clean stadium in Multan in 2004. To watch him bat to nobody was to take him out of his permanent context and follow just his game. And yet, I remember almost nothing of his innings. It went entirely as a matter of fact: friendly pitch, hot days, thick fast bowlers, Tendulkar hundred. In light of Virender Sehwag's treble, it was almost an apologetic affair; 'he's got so many, I might as well chip in.' At 194 it wasn't insubstantial.

The real story, of course, was Dravid - leading in place of Sourav Ganguly - declaring with Tendulkar on 194. At the press conference at the end of the day, Tendulkar said, with little obvious emotion, "Obviously, I'm a little disappointed, having got so close. I was aware that the declaration was just around the corner, but when it came, I was taken by surprise."

That was all it took. Soon I became aware of Tendulkar of India, and the vast machine that makes that so. Swiftly this beast whirred into action, too swift for something of that mass and size for the action to be particularly considered. All of India had a point to make. Ganguly had orchestrated the whole thing, of course he had, for he was Bengali and the grand manipulator of everything including the sun. Tendulkar's selfishness had finally been exposed. Dravid was not as *seedha* or *shareef* as he looked, something was up between him and Tendulkar. There had been a failure of communication. Tendulkar hadn't come out to field because he was upset. Everyone knew something, many eyebrows were raised, double-takes taken, winks and whispers offered. The noise was unlike any I'd heard.

Meaning was sought: What did it mean for India, this declaration, for it must mean something in this age where every action must have equal and opposite meaning? Tendulkar was so big that declaring on him was not just a captain's policy statement, it was a vision statement charting out a new future. Authoritative voices said it was the start of a new time. Team success, not individual glory, would now be important.

Parallels came to mind. Imran Khan declaring on Javed Miandad in 1982-83 in Hyderabad, with Miandad on 280, was one, though only a superficial one of captain denying his best batsman the chance of an individual landmark. The better parallel is an earlier one also from Imran, when he dropped his cousin Majid Khan in his very first Test as captain; to players that was a decision that signalled a change of culture, that merit and nothing else, would now matter.

The Tendulkar dilemma is an eternal one of team sport: fitting individual talent into a team structure to the harm of neither. With him it has been, at times, acute. Despite having several fine

Friends again after the match: With Pakistan's Inzamamul Haq and Sourav Ganguly.

batsmen alongside him from early in his career, hopes, odds, prayers and focus always rested most intensely on Tendulkar. His interests and fortunes have been those of India's; he scored runs, India scored runs and if he didn't, India usually didn't.

Multan, though, came during a time when India's Fab Five middle order (even if Ganguly was absent) was establishing itself as the best middle order around and among the best ever. Sehwag, Dravid, VVS Laxman and Ganguly meant there were others scoring big runs not just Tendulkar. The pressure was finally off, though with it went a little of the spotlight. His contribution, vital still, was no longer as critical, perhaps even no longer as feted as it once was. Sehwag, once a Tendulkar clone, was now just the freshest, most unique thing in batting, don't you know? Dravid had become the wall on which new India was built, Laxman the charm and magic to which it was irretrievably wedded. Ganguly had changed India altogether. Among the easy stereotypes where went Tendulkar?

Multan was, to me, about the adjustment back of a star to the galaxy around him. Tendulkar's comment, of which there was criticism, was an honest expression of personal disappointment. It was also a reflection of change and most intriguingly, the merest slip of the veneer of Tendulkar the icon to reveal Tendulkar the human. Not many stars as big as him have come to terms comfortably with any realignment of either their role in a side or their place in the lights. Yet many years from the event now, many runs, hundreds and wins later, is there any outward, even tiny sign that he has handled that in any way other than the best? Could he be one of the few subcontinent stars to retire right and grow old gracefully?

Pakistan, I suspect, would love to have Tendulkar as he was in Chennai in January 1999 every time. He fought the good fight that Test, a solitary one. His second-innings hundred had all in it to warrant appreciation – even if it might be grudging – across all divides of nationality. But that he couldn't take India over the line ultimately kept things in tidy, relieved balance; not quite Cardus wanting to watch a Trumper hundred as Australia crumbled to England, but more, in our unique dance of love and hate, Miandad hitting that last ball for two, or not hitting it at all in Sharjah. In this dance there is the recognition of a genuine master, even if he is from the enemy land. But there is also *schadenfreude* at his failure, because he is from the enemy land.

Chennai is particularly relevant for the manner of its denouement, of Tendulkar not leading India to a win. Here was more proof of his one perceived chink, a confused amalgam of his low fourth innings average and an inability to be there at the end when matches are won or lost. Pakistanis have latched on to this with particular conviction, without fail pulling out Inzamam-ul-Haq's remarkable matchwinning hundreds stat (17 of his 25 hundreds were in winning Tests; only 20 of Tendulkar's 50, by contrast).

If the numbers didn't prove it then there was always Imran's early decree – God-like as they all were – that Inzamam was the more talented batsman to fall back on, an assessment as open to shredding as most of Imran's woolly political thinking. And if, finally, you insist on recalling Inzamam's own poor record against the best bowling attacks of his day, Australia and South Africa, then there's always Brian Lara.

There is more to this than just the kind of childish envy you often come across in this relationship. Pakistan can rightly feel like the household that got away with only superficial damage in the midst of a hurricane as far as Tendulkar is concerned. No real, lasting scars were inflicted upon them by Tendulkar, none of the kind Miandad's six, for example, left.

There were occasions of course, the Multans and Centurions and Chennais, but over a 20-year career Pakistan takes a certain pride in his averages against them in all forms being considerably less than his career averages. And they probably chuckle at the men who have dismissed him most often. In the land of Imran and the Ws, the legend-lite troika of Abdul Razzaq, Azhar Mahmood and Aaqib Javed have had the most success against him in ODIs. Shoaib Akhtar and Saqlain Mushtaq have got him thrice each in Tests, but so has Shahid Afridi.

Mostly, Tendulkar's Indo-Pak experience has been an underwhelming one. Indeed a far deeper wound has already been left by Sehwag in the modern age; a treble, two doubles and a 90-plus Test average are taunts within which hide a particularly cruel, expressionless delight in ripping apart pace bowlers, the very heart of Pakistan's pride and chauvinism all these years.

Tendulkar's last visit to Pakistan, in 2006, was his worst. He scored 63 runs in a three-Test series infested with easy runs, troubled persistently by quick, short bowling. His only notable contribution was to tabloidism, his age and poor form the subject of the greatest headline ever involving Tendulkar, age and poor form: 'Endulkar?' A sub editor chuckled, a nation gasped and its neighbour sniggered. Four years, 40-plus Tests, over 3000 runs, thirteen 100s, fourteen 50s and a very modern 55-ish average later, only one man is laughing.

Tendulkar's place in his country is a place unoccupied by any player around the globe. For over twenty years he has been in this harsh space, which breaks a man wholly and comfortably. Yet, he's barely been scratched, as man, as batsman. He now has the most of everything, hundreds, runs, matches, money. Still he plays on, scoring doubles in ODIs, bouncing into the IPL like a fresh, unseen child, so clearly and purely in love with what he does.

He came at a time of great change in his country and perhaps became an agent for change in the country's cricket. He was, they said, the face for a new India on and off the field. That makes him now the old face of a newer India and somehow in essence he remains unchanged. Endurance and commitment are only heard about in their absence.

OSMAN SAMIUDDIN is the Pakistan editor of Cricinfo.

Their walks to the crease told the story. Richards used to wait till the vanquished had almost vanished. Perhaps he had been snoozing in the rooms - never sleeping, for he was too wary for that, too paranoid, felt that the world was against him and his kind and needed watching, a sensibility that could make him volatile, resenting every slight, even the imaginary. Nor did it take much to turn suspicion into conviction. His place, and the rage about it, was part of his driving force, gave him a reason to take an attack apart when statistics alone were not enough (which was most of the time).

Richards roused was a sight to behold. Consider his highest moments, the onslaught in '76 after Tony Greig said he wanted to make the West Indians grovel, the attacks on Bob Willis whose supposedly belittling remarks of years ago remained in his mind. Richards could not bat to score runs; the practice itself was not enough. There had to be a reason.

And so he'd stir himself as he prepared to enter the arena, dance a few steps, trying to break into a sweat. He admired Joe Frazier, welcomed his nickname of Smokin' Joe. Eventually he'd put on his cap and gloves and wend his way quickly through the crowd, hearing the breathless hush and then the roar as, head erect, chewing gum as another man might an enemy, he walked onto the field with a defiant swagger. It was an entrance.

For Tendulkar cricket is the cause

Tendulkar practices no such arts, does not seek to announce or shrivel or buoy himself or turn a park into a battleground. It is enough for him that cricket is a game, his favourite game. He does not need anything else. Always it has been the same. The most underestimated thing about him has been his longevity, his steadiness. Throughout twenty years of intense pressure and unrelenting exposure he has retained his delight. Through it all he has managed to focus on the next ball and the next innings. There have been no demons. Remaining simple is difficult and he has managed it. By no means is it the least of his contributions.

Perhaps it is that he has never stopped appreciating the game, never let it become a job or a chore. He enjoys cricket, and batting in particular. He'd play from dawn till dusk if they'd let him, and again the next day. Has any cricketer of his calibre changed less? Has any sportsman of his duration shown as few signs of mental wear and tear? Garry Sobers comes closest. For him, too, the game never became an ordeal. Of course the body grumbles but the Indian's mind has stayed forever young. To an extraordinary extent Tendulkar bats the same way and plays for the same reasons as in his youth. Its not that he has failed to grow; just that from the outset he saw the game in its true light, as an end in itself.

And it shows in his approach to the crease. It is the same as everyone else's, lacks all distinction. Richards nurtured majesty, Tendulkar leans towards the common man. Except that excitement builds around the ground as his name is put on the board, it might be another man emerging through the gate. Tendulkar takes the anticipation, and so much else, in his stride. It's absurd to think about him as a saint. A French philosopher once pointed out that "even the best amongst us, were all our deeds to be known, could not escape hanging ten times over." But he does bat without arrogance.

Perhaps, though, the modesty hints at a failing. According to the more exacting critics, Tendulkar does not often enough impose his will upon a match, dictate its outcome. Comparisons are made with the decisive innings played by Brian Lara and Richards himself.

Occasionally, it cannot be denied, Tendulkar has taken his team to the brink only to falter in the final frenzy. Yet it is a harsh judgement. No man has it all. For all his flamboyance, Lara did not transform let alone transcend. Just that his most scintillating innings were decisive and, too, linger in the mind, defining a brilliant, fitful career. Moreover West Indians often complain about his inconsistency. Unmatchable at his best, he was a frustrating and unreliable colleague.

Richards was an exuberant, overpowering force on the game's biggest stages. Proud and brave, he stamped his authority on proceedings. Team-mates at Somerset knew they just had to get him

With the ICC awards - Player of the Year 2010.

to Lord's and he'd take care of the rest. Often he did not contribute much in the early rounds. It was the same with the West Indies. His ability to seize the moment has seldom been equalled in any sport. In that regard he is the Indian's superior, and everyone else's.

Tendulkar was not like that. He'd expend as much energy in the early rounds as the later. The 2003 World Cup was a case in point. He revived a battered Indian team with a nerveless innings in Pietermaritzburg, thrillingly thrashed Shoaib Akhtar and company all around Centurion to take his team to the final and then failed in that match after the Australians had flogged a woebegone attack. Long before Tendulkar took guard the match was over, yet he was blamed.

In any case these high moments are only one aspect of the game. Richards' bad spells and periods of misadventure are too easily forgotten. He did not play against the greatest team of the era yet averaged only 50. That is not to deny him greatness, merely to frame it. That Tendulkar has occasionally faltered at critical moments pales beside his achievements. Moreover had his batting relied more on occasion and inspired emotion he might not have lasted half as long or been as productive or popular. Lara has been admired, Richards feared, Tendulkar cherished. A person must be taken all in. No man has everything. But to wish Tendulkar away is madness.

He did not need to search for meaning or motivation

Richards and Tendulkar also used the bat differently. In Richards' hand it was not a tool but a weapon. The niceties were not for him. He did not dwell upon technique. Despairing of his form, Eldine Baptists once sought his advice. Hours later he left with tears in his eyes. Richards did not say anything about cricket, told him instead what it means to be a man. To him cricket was a game of character not feet and elbow.

His batting was mostly instinctive. In 1973 he emerged as a lithe back foot player with a compelling cut and a thunderous drive. He made it look easy and partners were inspired. Of course then they did not know he was a genius, merely a talented young man. Adapting to English conditions, within two years he was stepping forward and across his stumps and flicking anything within reach through mid-wicket. Of course he could hook as well, in the West Indian way. By then he had become immensely fit and strong, the product of rigorous training. This was a time of youth and eye and conquest. Towards the end, not trusting himself quite as much, still wearing a cap but slower of reflex, dropping down the order as befitted an elder, he began to play more towards extra-cover, started to give himself time to settle.

Not that he lacked technique. Just that he wanted to dominate. Now and then he'd decide to subdue a few balls whereupon he'd produce immaculate, even exaggerated defensive shots. When he put his mind to it, though, he could score runs against any bowling on any pitch. Along the way he resisted Dennis Lillee and Bhagwat Chandrasekhar, and compiled a measured, masterful hundred against Derek Underwood on a crumbling county pitch. The latter innings was an essay in skill.

To compare Richard's batting with Tendulkar's is to put a culture against a civilisation. Tendulkar is a purist, in command of himself even amidst a withering attack, contemplative yet rarely hesitant, stylish yet not giving style more than it's due. He can concentrate without apparent effort and so does not need to summon any dark force to urge him along. He gives himself so completely to his activity that it becomes him. Batting is part of his essence. Richards was a performer, he is a player. Hence he scores as many runs in minor matches as on the great stages. It does not take an occasion to rouse him. He is stimulated by the activity itself.

Richards' bat was an expression of his personality; Tendulkar's willow is an extension of his being. His technique is well nigh flawless yet it is not the product of supreme dedication or endless application. According to the coaches of his youth, he could play all the shots correctly without instruction. From the start he understood the necessity, the advantages obtained from precise stroke play, realised that he could bat longer and score more runs by these means and so adopted them. And he found he could reproduce the shots that existed in his mind without undue difficulty. In that regard he resembled Mozart, a prodigy incapable even in childhood of producing an ugly note.

Almost from the outset Tendulkar could straight drive and cut and flick off his pads. Accordingly he batted ever longer on the matches held every morning on Shivaji Park. Even his shot selection was sound. Of course he made mistakes of execution but his judgement has seldom let him down. From Shivaji onwards it has merely been a matter of attention to detail and adding to his repertoire as the situation required. Throughout he has been a perfectionist. Indeed it has sustained him. After stumps he can sometimes be seen on the square, practising a hundred times the shot that had brought him down, often a back foot force demanding exact timing and footwork. It is an act of unconscious humility. Before series, too, he will anticipate the challenges that lie ahead, asking leg-spinners to pitch into the rough or else seeking a damp pitch to meet English conditions. He is a professional constantly in search of a better way. Always he thinks practically and positively. But his game does not undergo any substantial change. Natural and classical were interwoven at birth.

Now comes the question that is endlessly debated and beyond settlement. Of course it is idle to compare sportsmen from different. It is also irresistible. As far as batting is concerned, Richards and Gavaskar stood out in their era. Ricky Ponting notwithstanding, Tendulkar and Lara have shone brightest in the last two decades. Perhaps Richards' destructive powers put him higher even than his contemporary. Of the moderns, Lara could soar highest but Tendulkar has been his superior owing to the number of outstanding innings he has contributed.

Choosing between Richards and Tendulkar is the hardest task of them all. At present the Antiguan wallows in the warm glow of posterity, his flaws forgotten and long since forgiven. Tendulkar is still playing and so still open to inspection.

Suffice it to say that Richards has been the most withering, charismatic and exciting batsman to appear in the last 40 years. Suffice it to say that Tendulkar has been the most productive and satisfying to watch. Richards often disappointed. He batted on the edge of himself and the game. Danger was part of his attraction. Tendulkar has been classical and complete. And his achievement has been colossal. West Indies has not survived Richards; India has been uplifted by its hero.

Nor is it wise to scorn productivity. All those hundreds, all those shots beautifully executed. Throughout there has been a harmony in his game missing in the raging West Indian. There was anger in Richards, even violence, absent in the Indian.

Moreover Tendulkar has had much more on his plate, the expectations of millions, the match fixing scandal, the raising of a family. He has lasted the course better than anyone could reasonably have expected. Cricket is an exhausting game yet there has been no indication of anguish or ill health. Instead he has continued batting in his glorious way, thereby putting all else in its place.

All things considered Tendulkar has been the best of them all (excepting Bradman, who belongs in a category of his own). No one has played more breathtaking innings in the highest company, or scored more runs, or given more pleasure. To watch a Tendulkar straight drive is to observe the attainment of an ideal. The age, and occasionally the game itself, has belonged to him.

PETER ROEBUCK captained Viv Richards at Somerset. His books include It Never Rains, Tangled Up in White, *and* In It To Win It.

With Murali Vijay in the course of a 300 plus partnership against Australia.

SAHARA

SINGER

A LIFE IN ONE DAY

R Mohan

In that entire innings of 82 Sachin ran only one single for himself

True cricket lovers know that only once in a while does a day come along that is destined not to fade. Such a day shimmers in memory. One such day came in the eternally fresh air of New Zealand, in March 1994. It was to prove a seminal event in Indian cricket and historic for Sachin Tendulkar, the game's most complete batsman, which he could not have become if not for that very special day.

By then Sachin had played more than four years of international cricket and earned the thoroughly deserved reputation of being the best young batsman in the world. Great Test centuries in Sydney, Perth and Cape Town were the early bookmarks when he was already well on his way to becoming a Test great. He was, however, nowhere as accomplished in the limited-overs game.

The twin tests of greatness in the early modern era lay in meeting the demands of Tests and limited-overs cricket. Viv Richards was seen as the one who fulfilled the criterion best. After a tardy start, Sachin had shone spasmodically in ODIs, his calm innings against Pakistan in the World Cup in Sydney bearing the early signs of potential greatness in the important one-day arena.

His batting was probably as safe as that of a virgin at a convention of eunuchs. This tended to reflect in the ODIs too but we knew he was capable of far greater things there. Like it was said of Placido Domingo - considered the greatest opera singer of our time – that he had to return after decades as a tenor to his baritone roots to flirt with true grandness, Sachin also needed to find his métier.

He found it that day at the Eden Park in Auckland, famous for pitches that would flatten out during the day and be at their very best by early evening. But it took an accident in the form of a fitness problem for Sachin to open the innings. The rest, as they say, is history. But I must take a detour here to try and find the reason for Sidhu's stiff neck, strictly in the medical sense of course.

New Zealand is one of those idyllic places touring which is to be seen as a sort of working holiday for cricketers. Considering the vast time difference of seven and a half hours, to the press pack reporting from New Zealand is the nearest thing to legitimate theft. Even so, things can get a little dull out there unless you are privy to a large circle of Patels who monopolise the fruit and veggie business.

To wander through the city centre from nearby hotels is one way to pass the time. And from there to find the strip clubs is not a task beyond mortals far lesser than Captain Cook. I am not suggesting anything is amiss in brave young cricketers wishing to take in the sights of the cities they visit and the strip clubs of Auckland are sanitised versions of those that exist on the Hill in Sydney.

One night, probably the one before the match in question, we of the press pack trooped off to one of the clubs and had to wait to be let in for the night show. And who should troop out of the theatre at the end of the evening show but the Indian cricket team, led by its able manager! In the good old days of cricket, when men were expected to be men and the press was not so salaciously intrusive, a nightclub visit was seen as a fun thing.

Again, not for a moment, is it suggested that Sidhu craned his neck for a closer view of the huge flesh show. But, given the circumstances, his stiff neck became the butt of press box jokes before we were awakened mentally by the wondrous experience of watching the real Sachin, who unleashed the full extent of his batting prowess, in the literal as well as metaphysical sense.

It was a bit like the opening of Ali Baba's cave as the strokes flowing on the evening assumed a gem-like lustre. We saw the future that day when Sachin found his true calling. If striking the new ball is so easy and strokes fetch their highest reward with the field up, why did he not open the ODI innings before may well have been thoughts that struck the Little Master.

Promoting him had been thought of earlier, as in the rain-hit World Cup match against Zimbabwe in the same country a couple of years, but Kapil was pushed into the slot in a desperate situation. Sachin may have given the subject fleeting thought but the team always saw him as too valuable to be thrown against the hazards of striking out at the new ball, while his middle order presence suggested solidity.

In his one-day batting he always retained that child-like enthusiasm

In a late evening team meeting before the match, Sachin had put up his hand when the team was asking around about opening options if Sidhu could not take the field. Sachin's early strokes that afternoon after a New Zealand collapse carried not so much unusual belligerence as precision. They were simply fine cricketing strokes, which gained amazing value because of the field restrictions.

Why had Team India not given this matter serious thought earlier? Be that as it may, the game was given a whole new twist by a genius who found his true batting spot in the one-day order of things quite by accident. The New Zealand television had tipped off Indian journalists that they would be put on TV if they took vantage spots nearer the action and so some of us trooped out to near the edge of the boundary.

Watching Sachin from close up was even more thrilling than from a sterile press box perch where constant viewing of the television set tends to distort the real dimensions of a cricket field. From near the boundary rope, we marvelled more at the shots that came ringing off Sachin's bat – like mellifluous notes from a Yehudi Menuhin or a Lalgudi Jayaraman. In that entire innings of 82 (49 balls, 2x6, 15x4, a three, 3 twos) Sachin ran only one single for himself. This was amazing stuff and we did not need more proof about the great turning point having arrived.

What opening did to the master was to turn him quickly into a maestro and a batting phenomenon on whose adrenaline at the start of an innings a whole nation would swim or sink. Carrying the hopes of a billion never meant more in the literary and figurative sense.

Between the first century that came within months of his day in Auckland and the amazing 'Desert Storm' experience came many an innings that continued to define the new Tendulkar who had mastered the art of taking on the new ball bowlers at their freshest in limited-overs cricket. But none signified how much one man meant to his team and to his nation than the knocks he played in Sharjah when there were even doubts over whether India would make the final at all.

We said that day that if Sachin had wanted to stop the sandstorm from blowing, the elements would have obeyed. So complete was his command that the gods relented to allow play to resume while cricket's favourite son treated the bowlers with a disdain that bordered on the surreal.

At the dinner on the eve of the final, Steve Waugh was wondering aloud whether there was any way Sachin could be stopped. I said, "I am not even sure I should be telling you this. But if there are any weaknesses at all in his game now... the first is he tends to hit his cuts in the air and a very square third man might get a chance and the second is sometimes he tends to get inside the line to tickle to the left of the 'keeper. If you don't get him in the first five overs as he tries something extravagant, you will never get him."

Tears were shed on the night Sachin brought India to the brink of victory against Australia in Hyderabad

The issue may have been academic as I checked Waugh's field placement and found a square third man as well as a fine leg slip in over number one. Soon, one shot from Sachin screamed in the air towards deep point before falling safely short but never did he try to leg glance the quicks as India set off in pursuit of the target in the final. My nervousness eased soon as I did not want my silly comments leading to a Sachin dismissal in the final. But then he was, as they say, 'in the zone' again and fat chance the Aussies had of stopping him.

The safest batsman in the world had also begun satisfying his inner craving for being able to dominate bowling attacks. His innings against Pakistan at Centurion in the World Cup of 2003 was as unforgettable as it was cheekiness personified, with upper cuts flowing. One of the quickest bowlers in the world had been so tamed that he reacted with ferocity by virtually chucking the ball at the master to finally get him when he was just short of his century.

His Test batting may have gradually gone into a defensive mode with a few failures thrusting caution on him, as it happened so famously in his Sydney double hundred. In his one-day batting he always retained that child-like enthusiasm, his foremost quality that has endeared him to one and all. The carping critics who saw a few failures of his as a serial flunking in key matches like the World Cup final, may have no idea of what the success rate of openers is as they aim to strike out at the new ball.

The celebrations around his 20 years in international cricket were truly national. It was almost as if India was reaching some landmark like 60 years of Independence. How much of a national treasure he is was stressed in the emotions that were evoked by the landmark. And the Little Master rose to the occasion like a performer inspired by the atmosphere at a special occasion. His century in the chase against Australia had the nation on its feet.

Tears were shed on the night Sachin brought India to the brink of victory against Australia in Hyderabad. Just minutes earlier, his century had been welcomed with the kind of reception that may have been reserved for the midnight of the historic day in August 1947. As India revelled in his landmark it was as if the true value of a cherished icon had hit home. Sachin had evolved into a persona greater than the combined weight of his accomplishments on the field might suggest.

Kapil Dev sounded a lone and different note. He told me he was very disappointed that Sachin had not realised his 'true potential'. He made the point that Sachin was not making the big Test hundreds, that he was slowing down to be over cautious every time he passed 50 in Tests. He said a batsman of Sachin's calibre should be speeding up to very big scores in quick time after passing a milestone like a Test century. He also offered the opinion that Sachin was capable of making 200 in an ODI.

Prophetic words they proved and when I converted them into an Op-Ed page article for my newspaper in his name, Kapil complained bitterly that he should have written the piece himself. He said what he actually meant when he talked about Sachin not realising his 'true potential' would have come out better had he penned the words. As luck would have it, Sachin decided to prove one of the legends of Indian cricket right. He went and made a double century in an ODI and raised the bar to a nearly impossible height for future generations.

Months after the feat its enormity is yet to sink in. I know batsmen have been close enough to defying the Saeed Anwar, milestone for a while now. For Sachin to get there before the crippling muscle cramp and dehydration set in at the ripe age of 36 made the accomplishment all the more remarkable. This was no colt sprinting away to a Derby triumph. The greatest thoroughbred who shone on the longest events was now showing it has the speed too.

No batsman in history could ever have been so complete a batsman. Some may still crib at the distance he keeps from the T20 but this is a considered decision taken on the eve of the first World T20 championship. Every time he shows his capacity for T20 speed, people start pressuring him to play for India in the international version. The master will not relent. He has nothing left to prove.

When will history see such a complete batsman again? From Bradman through Richards we have moved on to a performer who has beaten everyone in terms of centuries, runs and endurance. And he has done all this without letting anyone see his private life. In an intrusive age, he has kept his life to himself while still being the icon to a billion people. Never once has he misbehaved on the field of play, never been demonstrative at the injustice that sometimes seemed to be aimed particularly at him.

A job he loves.

What we see in him is a fantastic combination of qualities all too rare even in sportsmen with a tunnel vision for whom life may just be the sport and events around it. And his modesty has always forbidden him from speaking aloud about his cricket. Only in the last World Cup in which he was said to have gone into his shell because he was not asked to open the innings did he ever seem to place self above team.

It is remarkable that he has got better with age, right down to running between the wickets. Two decades after his debut he is still a match winner of the highest quality. 'If he leads Indian batting in the World Cup and takes India anywhere near the summit he would have done more single-handedly than many for his nation'. We look forward to what might be his really last big chance on the biggest cricket stage at the World Cup. If he realises his ambition of being in a World Cup winning team, he would also be enlivening the lives of a billion people.

R MOHAN is Resident Editor of Deccan Chronicle *and* Wisden's *India correspondent.*

THE 'SYMBOLICAL' CRICKETER

Mike Marqusee

His low centre of physical gravity is matched by a low centre of psychological gravity, making him much harder to topple

"Cricket is first and foremost a dramatic spectacle," wrote CLR James in *Beyond a Boundary*. "It is so organised that at all times it is compelled to reproduce the central action which characterises all good drama from the Greeks to our own: two individuals are pitted against each other in a conflict that is strictly personal but no less strictly representative of a social group."

Where "the dramatist, the novelist, the choreographer must strive to make his individual character symbolical of a larger whole," in cricket that "symbolical" quality is inherent. "The batsman facing the ball does not merely represent his side. For that moment, to all intents and purposes, he is his side. This fundamental relation of the One and the Many, Individual and Social, Individual and Universal, leader and followers, representative and ranks, the part and the whole, is structurally imposed on the players of cricket."

In the case of Sachin Tendulkar, that representative, "symbolical" function has been exponentially compounded. I like to imagine him roaring around a late night Mumbai in one of his flashy cars, revelling in the surrounding darkness, the emptiness, the anonymity. Free of the burdens of representation. Able to be, for a moment, not the One who must bat for the Many but merely one among many.

I was travelling in India in the autumn of 1989 and followed the mounting excitement over the 16-year-old batting phenomenon. At the time, having watched a succession of talents traumatised by teenage celebrity, I worried whether any youngster could survive such attention and expectation without damage.

Since then, the pressures of sports-stardom have intensified. Can we be sure that the geniuses of the past would have been able to sustain their best form in the relentless glare of today's celebrity culture? Or that they would have succeeded in negotiating the numerous pitfalls accompanying a degree of wealth and renown previously undreamed of?

The art of letting it go.

It has been argued that Tendulkar is the beneficiary (and victim) of an Indian culture of hero-worship, but this theory severs Tendulkar from his times and therefore obscures his significance. His career coincides with the rise of neo-liberal India and its competitive, aspirational ethic. For the class of Indians that in these years entered and embraced the global consumer culture, Tendulkar became a powerful signifier. If Sachin hadn't existed, India would have had to invent him. The dominant culture of the day demanded an icon of success.

This success has been seen as simultaneously 'individual' and 'national'. Tendulkar's personal achievements were represented as a triumph for India as a whole, a sign of the country advancing on the world stage - like Indian corporations opening plants in Europe or the USA. Unwittingly and unwillingly, he found himself at the epicentre of a popular culture shaped by the intertwined growth of a consumerist middle class and an assertive, sometimes aggressive form of national identity. National aspirations and national frustrations were poured into his every performance, and this during a period in which the nation passed through some very dark moments (Kashmir since 1989, Ayodhya in 1992, Mumbai in 1993, Gujarat in 2002, Mumbai in 2009). How he's not been crushed by it all remains at least in part a mystery.

Tendulkar has been a modern man playing in a modern style in the modern marketplace - and that's what makes him of supreme importance to Indians. He's a home-grown genius excelling in a transcontinental spectacle, a high-value icon of personal success in a globalised economy, a world-beater bred in the heart of Mumbai's status-hungry middle class. Yet he's survived largely untainted by the turmoil, factionalism, jealousy and corruption surging around him.

Tendulkar must be one of the least criticised of all modern super-stars. No other figure of remotely comparable celebrity has been treated so kindly by the media and the fans. Gavaskar and Kapil Dev, not to mention Azharuddin and Ganguly, his predecessor and successor as Indian captain, all had much rougher rides. As did Warne, Lara and Muralitharan, not to mention Amitabh Bachchan, Shah Rukh Khan, Tiger Woods, Michael Jordan or David Beckham. Tendulkar has never been subject to the kind of detraction, justified or not, which all these others have suffered.

Why should that be? For a start, Tendulkar has been careful to make no enemies and give no offence. He has accepted the friendship of every political party and refused none. Despite his exalted status, he knows his place as a sports star and has been careful not to overstep its bounds. Playing cricket has always seemed his exclusive priority. His occasional poor spells may have raised concerns but no one suggested he was distracted, arrogant or indifferent. The modest demeanour is said to be unaffected, but it has also served well as a personal survival strategy. It enables him to avoid controversy and thereby apply himself exclusively to the one battle he really cares about: against the opposing bowlers.

For non-Indians
the joy of Tendulkar
comes unadulterated

What's more, India (and the larger cricket world) wants and needs Tendulkar to be pure, innocent, transcendent. Somehow he has managed to absorb that mass projection and reflect it back; he stands solidly on his pedestal. Sachin started young but unlike many others he's managed to stay young. It's clear he takes an unadulterated joy in playing cricket, in solving the endless problems it poses, ball after ball. Cricket has always been his primary means of self-expression, so absorbing, so efficient that he hasn't needed to assert himself in other ways.

Cricket commentary is filled with psychological platitudes: we mutter about 'competitiveness,' 'determination,' 'confidence' and counter-pose them to anxiety, self-doubt or timidity. We take these polarised categories for granted, assuming that one leads to success and the other to failure, though experience teaches us otherwise. It is always more complicated than that. Among cricketers, confidence and doubt are layered one upon another. When Tendulkar bats, there is confidence aplenty, but also introspection and circumspection. The confidence is without swagger. Tendulkar dominates but, unlike Viv Richards, rarely domineers. His low centre of

Sharing a garland with icons Gavaskar, Vishwanath and thespian Amitabh Bachchan.

physical gravity is matched by a low centre of psychological gravity, making him much harder to topple.

As the inheritor of the venerable Mumbai tradition of cultivated batsmanship, Tendulkar has seamlessly blended power and grace, efficiency and elegance, conscientious craftsmanship and quicksilver improvisation. Calculation and spontaneity are impossible to distinguish. That's what makes his style classical: technique is grafted to imagination.

A great run-maker in both the Test and one-day formats, he stands at the intersection of the old and the new; through him we have seen one enrich the other. He paved the way for the contemporary masters of one day cricket not by abandoning his Test technique but by amplifying and accelerating it, opening the field to a wider variety of strokes. His average in the course of five World Cups stands at 57.93 – with a strike rate higher even than Viv Richards'.

But among Tendulkar's numerous statistical achievements, it's his record number of Test hundreds, one in every five and a half Test innings, that is the most impressive and may prove the most durable. Hundreds shape matches; they set up victories or stave off defeats. More than that, the compilation of a Test hundred is an art in itself, unique and demanding - because of the time it takes and because it requires mastering different bowlers with different styles, as well as changing field placings, weather and ball conditions, not to mention shifting partners at the other end. It demands an eye ever alert to the ball that's not quite good enough, and equally to the one that's too good. A Test century is a feat of stamina and concentration, but also of vision: comprehending in single moments (again and again) the many possibilities in time and space embodied in the approaching ball. These qualities Tendulkar has possessed in abundance.

But for reasons that remain hard to fathom, his tenure as captain was deeply disappointing. He seemed to have all the qualifications: an exceptional cricket brain, an even temperament, the respect of his fellow players. What's more he led a strong side featuring the likes of Dravid, Ganguly, Kumble and Srinath. Yet in his 25 Tests in charge, he won only 16 percent and lost 36 percent, compared to Azharuddin's record of just under 30 percent won and 30 percent lost and Ganguly's of 43 percent won and 26 percent lost. His record as an ODI captain was even worse: winning only 35 percent of his matches in charge, compared to Azhar's 54.1 percent and Ganguly's 53.9 percent. Clearly being a 'symbolical' representative is not the same as being an effective leader. What was missing? His own batting suffered, but only marginally (his average as Test captain was over 50). The real problem was an inability to bring the team to the boil at the right time, to convert temporary advantages into winning positions.

Perhaps the very qualities that enabled him to survive in the spotlight muted and subdued him as a captain. Great captains need personalities with an edge (not necessarily aggressive but at least authoritative); they impose an emotional tone on the team, which helps to make the whole greater than the sum of the parts. Because Tendulkar was without edge, he seemed to lack a lever with which to pry open his team's talents.

One of the foibles of his captaincy was that he under-bowled himself, an error corrected by his successor, for whom he bowled more overs and took more wickets at a much lower strike rate (in both forms of the game). Unlike his batting, his bowling owed little to natural ability and nearly everything to cunning. That mix of off-breaks, leg-breaks and donkey drops appeared innocuous, but its mildness could mislead skilled batsmen into horrendous errors. It was always fun to watch.

Does Tendulkar have a dark side? I find it hard to believe that a life of so much creative energy, driven intensity, constant combat (ball after ball) could exist without its demons. Maybe they emerge from hiding during those pre-dawn drives along the Arabian Sea?

For non-Indians like myself, the joy of Tendulkar comes unadulterated. The awe he inspires belongs to no culture, carries no national overtones, and is both intimately personal and transparently universal. One of the major pleasures of watching competitors like Tendulkar is the sensation of awe they evoke. There is so much he does with ease that the rest of us can never hope to accomplish, even with prolonged and scientific training. The great thing here is that this awe does not leave us feeling belittled or inadequate.

On the contrary, the wonder and marvel at what one of our fellow human beings can do is expansive, life-enhancing: the intricate coordination of mind and matter, the welding together of eyes, feet and hands in the heat of the moment, all driven by a single competitive purpose, yet somehow making a thing of beauty beyond that single purpose. At their best, great sporting geniuses challenge and extend our notion of what is humanly possible. Normally when this happens outside the sporting realm, it is experienced as disturbing or threatening, but somehow, within cricket's redemptively trivial domain, it is irresistibly seductive.

So thank you, Sachin Tendulkar, for giving me as many of those invigorating awe-filled moments as any sporting genius of my time.

Mike Marqusee is the author of Anyone But England, Wicked Messenger: Bob Dylan and the Sixties, *and* Redemption Song, *a study of Muhammad Ali.*

187

SAHARA
Airtel

GO FIGURE

Suresh Menon

It is always the next milestone that is important, the one barely visible in the distance

Let's start with W.H. Auden. In his elegy to Sigmund Freud the poet wrote: *To us he is no more a person/now but a whole climate of opinion/under whom we conduct our different lives.* In India, Sachin Tendulkar ceased being a person long ago. To a small group of friends and colleagues he is human, with all the frailties that state implies. But to the vast majority he is merely a figure on television, indistinguishable from characters such as Superman, Batman and Hanuman.

When he does well, his fans go out and buy the toothpaste, the pain reliever, the insurance policy or whatever he is endorsing at the moment. When he fails occasionally - to remind everybody he is flesh and bone after all - they call for his head, write letters to newspapers saying he has been hanging on for too long, declare that he is too selfish and ought to make way for a younger man. Then he scores again and the wheel is set in motion once more. The cycle of birth and rebirth is never seen more clearly and more often than on the cricket fields of India.

Auden's lines say it well. Being a non-person means that your ambitions are not your own. Others decide how many runs you should make before you retire. The climate of opinion is both conducive to change and change itself. And these ambitions change with achievement. It is always the next milestone that is important, the one barely visible in the distance.

Sometimes the great man surprises his most ardent fan, with achievements beyond even their imagination. Two months short of his 37th birthday, he scores one-day cricket's first double century. Now the fans have to reset their sights. A century of international centuries is taken for granted; the only question is, when?

When Tendulkar began his career as a 16-year-old, satisfaction meant 35 centuries and 10,000 runs. Now that he is long past those figures, he has been issued with new targets. Just as a goal is reached, someone moves the goalposts. Anything fewer than 15,000 runs and 50 Test centuries will count as failure. He is nearly there. Once, that target is achieved the call will be to score 20,000 runs in ODIs. The charm of round numbers: as seductive to the sportsman as to his fans.

If it was King Eurystheus who set the tasks for Hercules of myth to perform, then it is the democratic voice of the people which is setting the tasks for the modern Hercules with his divine straight drive and fiery square cut.

"Sunil Gavaskar has told me that I have to get to 15,000 runs," Tendulkar once said. "He said he would be angry with me and would come and catch me if I didn't." The last part of that sentence is a literal translation from the vernacular. Roughly, it means "would chase me to the ends of the earth and make my life a living hell . . ."

With over 14,000 runs in Tests and 17,000 in ODIs, is Tendulkar satisfied looking down from the peak he alone occupies? His words are music to his fans' ears and a warning to bowlers everywhere: "I'm not pleased yet with what I have done."

Those who specialise in reading between the lines have seen the message and spread it: What a happy coincidence! Tendulkar's ambition is the same as the target his fans have on his behalf. He will be unhappy with anything less. And dissatisfaction is at the root of all progress and records. True or not, it is one of those statements that become fact on repetition; and when Tendulkar gets to the mark, there will be an inevitability about it that was not apparent earlier. That is the power of the self-fulfilling prophecy.

Scoring the 14,000th run.

You play long enough, noted Allan Border who was slightly embarrassed at the fuss made over his crossing the 11,000-run mark, “and you are bound to break a few records.”

“Tendulkar has set benchmarks for guys like me to chase,” Ricky Ponting has said. “If I had to last 20 years, I would probably be batting in a wheelchair.”

For years, the debate was Tendulkar versus Lara. Apollo versus Dionysius. The man who couldn’t put a foot wrong and the man who got away with indiscretions. Then Don Bradman

settled the issue, declaring from Olympian heights: Tendulkar is like me. No arguments. A decade and more after that pronouncement came another debate. Tendulkar versus Ponting. There is no batsman alive who can settle that with Bradmanesque certainty. So the argument is thrown open to statisticians. Forget the style, focus on the number. Ignore the impact, add up the runs.

In an era when greatness is adulterated by figures, there is concern that the cliché "records are made to be broken" may not hold. It is possible that whoever finishes with the most centuries and the highest aggregate in Test cricket will keep those records until the sun burns itself out. And that explains the intensity of the race - if not between the players themselves then among the respective fans.

This is partly due to the apprehensions over the future of Tests and the possible reduction in the number of matches played. Batsmen, like detectives in a murder mystery, look for means, motive and opportunity. It has to be all three - any two will not do. They can have the means or the ability to get the runs, but without the opportunity of playing Tests that will amount to nothing. Or they might have the opportunity, but without the motive or the means they will not trouble the statisticians. Then, since we are speaking of sport, there is the vexed question of age. The spirit may be willing, but if the flesh is close to 40, the future may be behind you.

Once someone makes 15,000 runs, it will be like mountaineering after Everest. There will be no more worlds to conquer. Unless, of course, cricket authorities everywhere go out of their way to keep Test cricket alive (instead of leaving it to market forces) with a specific number of matches allotted to each country. Possible, but hard to imagine.

For someone to make 15,000 runs, he would need to begin early (Tendulkar started at 16) and play through two decades averaging between eight and 10 Tests per year. That would mean keeping free of injury and scoring with a consistency to ensure an average in the mid-50s.

In the Tendulkar versus Ponting debate, we assume that the winner will touch the 15,000-mark soon. It makes calculations easier. It gives the players a definite target to aim at, although Ponting could retire tomorrow and Tendulkar might decide to focus on the World Cup alone. "I hit runs for my country," Ponting has said with all the diplomacy and quote-carefulness of a Tendulkar. "And when my career is over, I can reflect on the successes."

When Geoff Boycott, who had made a fetish of avoiding India in his playing days, toured in 1981-82 just so he could surpass Sobers' then world-record aggregate, he was told by Gavaskar after the event, "Enjoy it while you can." The Indian was close on his heels and would overtake him soon. Will Ponting be saying something similar to Tendulkar (if not publicly, at least in his mind)?

There is a question I'm asked often by Tendulkarites: will the Board allow him to play on till he makes 15,000 runs or 16,000 or 20,000? Some suggest that there ought to be a national campaign to ensure that the Indian icon gets to the mark. It is difficult to imagine the Australian board carrying Ponting until an individual milestone is reached. That is not its sporting culture. The manner in which Steve Waugh was asked to pack up and leave is more the Aussie way.

If Ponting is struggling and finds no place in the team but ends a series on 14,999 runs, it is unlikely that Australia will suddenly organise an out-of-turn series against Bangladesh to enable him to get that crucial single.

There will be a national outcry in India if Tendulkar were to be in the identical situation. Opinion-makers who don't know a leg slip from a cover drive will wax eloquent over denying a champion his true place in the sun. Television channels will run special programmes for weeks and get all manner of "experts" to testify that such behaviour is "just not cricket."

Indian cricket is based on passion, on easily-stirred emotions; players are worshipped for what they do, romance trumps realism, sentiment pushes out logic and reason. Performances are often taken out of context and enjoyed without any thought to their frame of reference. A Tendulkar ton in defeat is feted more heartily than a 40 in victory. That is why few are concerned that only 20 of Tendulkar's 50 Test centuries have been in winning causes.

Batsmen, like detectives in a murder mystery, look for means, motive and opportunity

To be able to appreciate a single performance in isolation, divorced from effect, unmindful of its place in the larger scheme of things might be a gift - but it is usually consolation for lack of a good team record overall. For generations, Indian fans have been consolation-seekers, venerating individual achievement above team result, and treating triumph and disaster in the manner recommended by Mr. Kipling.

If Tendulkar decides to play on, there is nothing likely to stop him - not the selectors, not the state of Indian cricket in general, not the changed circumstances should India slip steadily from its No. 1 position. This is a freedom denied to an Australian player, whatever his record, so Ponting will have to fit into the national team without upsetting its balance as age catches up with him.

There is, too, Tendulkar's own mindset. He is not a record-chaser by temperament but, given a choice after a long series, he would still rather play cricket than do anything else. His obsession has only grown despite the number of days he spends in a year playing international cricket. There has never once been a suggestion of staleness or satiation. Cricket is what he knows, and he has already hinted that retirement is not something he can bear to contemplate.

He will play on, not because there is a record at stake but because he loves to play on and on. But even such enthusiasm has to come up against Father Time. If Tendulkar has to reduce the number of days he plays just so he can increase the number of years he does so, it is likely that he will give up one-day cricket and focus exclusively on the traditional game. This is even more likely to happen should India win the 2011 World Cup. It has been a gap in the great man's bio-data - that the finest batsman in the history of the shorter game does not have a World Cup win to show for it. Viv Richards has two, Ponting three.

There is a picture of a three-year-old Tendulkar, shirtless and long-haired, in stance. The front leg is straight, the toes slightly open while the back knee is slightly bent. But what is remarkable is the grip on the bat, the top hand straight out of the manual, the back of the wrist facing the bowler (or photographer, actually). The eyes are dancing with a rare delight, the overall mood emphasised by a teeth-displaying smile. Clearly, this boy was born to play the game—and enjoy it too, passing on the pleasure to millions of fans.

By 15, he had made his first-class debut with a century for Mumbai, at 16 he was playing for India and at 17 was good enough to make a century in England. By 19 he had two tons in Australia and was anointed the best batsman in the world by hard-nosed writers who are not easily impressed.

The son of a teacher, Tendulkar had more than 3Rs drilled into him - there was Restraint and Righteousness and a couple of other things, too. Tendulkar worked hard at preserving his image. Indians expect their heroes to be soft-spoken, modest achievers.

Over the next few years, the subtext of all competition involving Tendulkar and Ponting will be the race. Both players are in the position of the man who does good by stealth and then has it found out by accident. They would like to play on, accumulating runs for the team which will incidentally put them on the top of the list. They are both competitive enough to appreciate the significance of this possibly unbreakable record.

I'm not pleased yet with what I have done/and when my career is over, I can reflect on the successes.

Not quite Auden, but in a strange way the two lines from different men in different corners of the world in response to varied questions seem to be saying the same thing.

SURESH MENON is one of India's most widely travelled writers. A version of this essay first appeared in Sports Illustrated.

OPUS

BLOOD, SWEAT AND TEARS

Gideon Haigh

A cricketer of Gandhian self-denial and Anandian self-containment

The Tendulkar blood book: it is surely the cricket freak story of the year. The impresarios behind Tendulkar's forthcoming autobiography, *Tendulkar Opus*, have commissioned an extra-limited limited edition of ten into which drops of the great man's blood will be mixed on the signature page. The other pages of the 37kg tome will be trimmed in gold leaf too, but it's the corpuscles and platelets that will be the selling point of the volumes priced at $75,000 each and....oh, hang on, sorry, they've already been sold, sight unseen.

'Only in America,' people used to groan at one of those news stories about some Bible Belt ecstatic who'd seen the face of Christ in a tortilla, or some millionaire eccentric who'd had the head of their favourite dog cryogenically frozen. 'Only in India,' is the modern-day cricket equivalent, the country being a byword for an ecstatic cricket rapture that makes the enthusiasm of other countries look mild - all effigy burnings, crazy television, eye-bulging bling, and Bollywood glamour.

Yet how often it is, even in the era of 'Captain Cool' Dhoni and/or 'See Ball, Hit Ball' Sehwag, that the Tendulkar stories trump them all, like the teenager who committed suicide a few years back when Tendulkar's back injury threatened to end his career, or the plot to kidnap him hatched by Pakistani terrorists? "The key thing here is that Sachin Tendulkar to millions of people is a religious icon," said the mastermind of the Tendulkar blood book. "And we thought how, in a publishing form, can you get as close to your god as possible?" Dhoni, Sehwag, Ganguly, Kumble – superstars all, but earthbound. Of only Tendulkar can you speak in terms of God and religion, and even then you might still be guilty of understatement. Perhaps the reason that the Indian cricket board has been so reluctant to sign up to the WADA (World Anti-Doping Agency) code is the probability of a black market in vials of Tendulkar's other secretions.

The most intriguing aspect of the Tendulkar Opus is not the ten copies that almost nobody will ever see but the thousands they will. At 852 pages, it will bulk larger even than Steve Waugh's personal apologia: another big record for the Little Master. What will it reveal? Easier to imagine what it will not. Lovechild? Lifelong battle with depression? Daily telephone banter with Shobhan Mehta? There'd be bloodshed then, and it wouldn't be the profitable kind. Actually, it's hard to conceive of what the book can disclose without causing the kind of controversy which to Tendulkar is anathema. Let's be frank: expect lots of respectful hat tipping to famous rivals, reverent and touching glimpses of family, maybe the odd behind-the-scenes story of Team India, but with an overall impression as enigmatic as the Mona Lisa's smile.

Nobody will feel genuinely let down either, for Tendulkar has so conditioned us. "I have taken stands before, but often whatever I say gets misinterpreted and meanings are attached to it," he has complained. "If you know that whatever you say will become a controversy, why get into it unnecessarily?" The best cricketer of his generation, in fact, has been among the least scandalous, keeping his head while all about him have not just been losing theirs but throwing them high in the air. Not for him the talk show couch, or the newspaper pulpit; while he is no longer the stilted youth of his first few television advertisements, cameras still seem to embarrass him slightly, and one would no sooner expect a cheesy product placement from him than a casual doosra.

Tendulkar has never 'spoken out' in cricket contexts

India has been transformed in his cricket lifetime, from a supplicant at the IMF to its modern tiger economy. So has the country's media, once staid and dowdy, now served by 125 24-hour television news services and more than 1100 TV channels, ravening for content and contention. Tendulkar's phlegmatism is sometimes contrasted to the flamboyance of his contemporary and boyhood companion Vinod Kambli, a batsman extravagantly gifted whose head was turned by adulation and celebrity. Kambli, it is averred, had talent to burn, and did; Tendulkar kept his nose not only clean, but to the grindstone. The comparison is flawed: Kambli was never that good; Tendulkar never that reticent. But they aren't the worst antitypes. When it has counted, Tendulkar has been preternaturally focused, a cricketer of Gandhian self-denial and Anandian self-containment.

Not that he has been altogether Sphinx-like. Look back in the annals and you will find that Tendulkar grants interviews quite regularly, or as regularly as one could reasonably expect in the absence of any great economic incentive for his doing so. In some of these interviews, he even goes into detail, at least about his batting, exhibiting a flair for succinct expression. Take this for example: "The mind always wants to be in the past or the future; it rarely wants to be in the present. My best batting comes when my mind is in the present, but it doesn't happen naturally. You have to take yourself there." Or this: "The older I get the more I realise how important your breathing is to good batting. By that I mean, if you focus on breathing and relaxing, you can force yourself into a comfortable place to bat." Not hugely original, but mature and reflective. Tendulkar on batting: it's not quite as good as Tendulkar batting, but there's substance to it, and an intelligence behind it.

As far as his fans are concerned, too, Tendulkar has been consistently generous. He is a quiet supporter of charitable and philanthropic causes, including Apnalaya, a Mumbai-based NGO assisting underprivileged children associated with his mother-in-law, Annabel Mehta. This year he even harnessed the internet as a means of scattering his blessings and benedictions, acquiring 88,000 followers within a day of his joining Twitter; that number now exceeds half a million. It is difficult to imagine that he personally sits there all day attending individually to his well-wishers – 'Thanx. Good luck to u n ur family. I wish u all the best in life'; 'Wish u good luck in life. Keep smiling'; 'Thanx a lot. I m humbled. Wish u n ur family all the good health n happiness in life' etc – but easy to imagine how such apparently personal confirmations are individually received. The Tendulkar tweet is to India as the Bradman autograph is to Australia: they abound, but somehow each one is special.

With childhood friend Vinod Kambli.

Of Tendulkar's views on other subjects, however, we know little or nothing - which may not, of course, be any great loss. A story is told, probably apocryphal, about an interview in the 1980s in which pop idol Kylie Minogue was asked her opinion of South Africa, possibly with the intent of extracting an undertaking she would not play Sun City. "I think they should stop shooting the rhinos," La Minogue is reputed to have replied, on the basis of some half-remembered wildlife documentary. From fame cannot be inferred a natural flair for entering into public debate; indeed, the contrary may be true, that fame entails such concentration on the self as to preclude profound interest in most other matters.

But Tendulkar has never 'spoken out' as he might have in cricket contexts, in the issues-rich environments of the nineties and noughties, when the game has been menaced by match-fixing, sledging, ball-tampering, illegal actions, administrative incompetence, greed and corruption. Did he not share with fans the pangs of hurt, of disappointment, of disgruntlement at cricket's travails? Did he not feel incited to a calming, diplomatic word, or even an expression of some sort of moral code?

One reason he perhaps did not is the fastidiousness with which he has quarantined his cricket life from the time he devotes to wife Anjali, and children Sara and Arjun. "When I cross the boundary line, it's not cricket, it's family," he has explained. "And when I think about cricket, it's only cricket." Given Tendulkar's single-mindedness at the crease, one can imagine the cordon sanitaire around his sport. He famously does not consume news media about his own performances; it would be a departure from type were he to consume news media concerning other issues.

Chances are, too, that he may not be particularly interested. The cricketer of Tendulkar's time has needed to cultivate a high tolerance for boredom: nets, hotels, departure lounges, airliners. Another hundred throwdowns? Suppose I'd better. Another hundred catches? Might help. It's not an environment conducive to broad perspectives or piercing visions, but to highly selective and heavily concentrated effort. If Tendulkar has kept his eye on his own particular ball, it may be because those other balls do not directly aid him in his superordinate goals of making runs and winning matches.

The predominant reason, however, is that hinted earlier: because it has simply never been worth it. Here is a man who cannot go shopping or dine in restaurants because of the inevitability of public interruption. Here is a man who experiences freedom most while driving around Mumbai in the wee hours of the morning. Here is a man who in public must adopt disguises and false beards lest the discovery of his presence cause a riot – one a few years ago, which involved 10,000 people in Bangalore, required 200 police to control it. When such unswerving intensity of attention is a fact of life, who would not wish to avert it at every opportunity? Balzac once ruminated of his fame that he wished it permitted him 'to break wind in society, and society would think it a most natural thing'. Tendulkar breaking wind in society today would hit India like a monsoon.

Every hero says something about their times, and perhaps this is one of the silent commentaries Tendulkar passes on his era, that the media and public are so conditioned to a climate of constant controversy, exaggeration and misrepresentation that participation is hardly worth the candle. Your view can be thoughtful, nuanced, lightly-held, tentatively-expressed, but after simplification and amplification by the various modern apparatus it will sound like a combination of abuse, insult and battle cry. If it is not in Tendulkar's nature to initiate such a process, then perhaps he is saner than the rest of us.

Perhaps, in fact, it is partly the ridiculousness of his world that has kept Tendulkar going so long: the pleasure, relief and solace cricket provides him in his splendid isolation. For here is the paradox of his extraordinariness - his making light of challenges on the cricket field that would daunt even very good international cricketers, while shrinking from the everyday experiences that seem simplest. Murali on a turning wicket, Steyn on bouncy one? Bring them on. Hundred to win in the last 10 overs of an ODI? He can feel his sap rise.

Cricket? He has done it before, and never seems to tire of the idea of repeating himself. But driving round the block? Walking down the street? Taking his children to the park or the beach? No way; not now; maybe never. And given the value imputed to his bodily fluids by Opus, Tendulkar cutting himself shaving should almost be covered in the business pages. Hang on again...I shouldn't make jokes like that, because it's perfectly possible that one day it will.

GIDEON HAIGH, historian of the game, is the author of Mystery Spinner *and* The Big Ship.

AHARA
187

AIR TENDULKAR

Barney Ronay

Tendulkar is a generous icon. He inspires a very personal kind of reverence

Sachin Tendulkar has been voted the greatest cricketer of all time by a landslide result in an Australian newspaper poll. According to the published results, 84 percent of those who expressed a preference believe Tendulkar has now overtaken Sir Donald Bradman as cricket's defining star, its Elvis, its Marilyn Monroe, its complete works of William Shakespeare.

Until recently this news would have elicited from me a kind of wincing, squinting chafing at the cerebral lobe that controls the urge to enter into ill-advised and unwinnable contrarian debates. Even in the same week that Tendulkar also became the first batsman to score 14,000 Test runs, while returning at the age of 37 to the top of the Test Match rankings, there might still have been a residual sense that there is perhaps something a little too corporate and earnest, too Princess Diana Memorial Book of Condolence, about the public outpourings of Tendulkar-worship that have tended to surge across the cricketing superstructure like shutter-battering weather fronts in monsoon season.

For me, Tendulkar has long represented a personal conundrum. There has always been something innately baffling about his peculiar brand of high-end excellence, right from the moment he first appeared in England, gliding to an oddly frictionless first Test century as 17-year-old at Old Trafford on India's 1990 tour. That first glimpse was indicative of what was to come: an innings of such flawless quality it seemed Tendulkar had arrived ready-formed, pre-tested and roadworthy, bereft of the alluringly ragged edges of youth.

Sure, since then I've trilled and cooed along with the rest of them, taking pleasure in a spotless double ton here, a mathematical dissection of the offside field there; all the while, though, furtively studying the swooning faces for a tiny hint of doubt, or at least for a sense of sober approval, or at least simple admiration, rather than the usual full-blown Tendul-itis.

This may seem churlish, but high praise is being doled out here and there is no upper limit to the demands we place on our Greatest-of-All-Timers. Even if, in the process, this involves a little tousling and chafing, a winningly rough edge to go with all that elite fine-tuning.

SAHARA
Airtel

This is the thing, you see. Watching Tendulkar often seemed to be an experience of such annihilating perfection, like being asked to admire an inconceivably well-engineered German supercar. It is a criticism, not of his batting style or tempo, but of its texture and temperature. In particular, mid-period Tendulkar had a Terminator-ish feel for me, an air of unblinking, calculus-level excellence, backed by the devouring quicksand of his unanswerable numbers. And what stats they are. Just look at that one day record. To date Tendulkar has 46 One Day International hundreds. The current England one day team has 16 between then. In fact, in the years since Tendulkar scored his first one day hundred in 1994 the entire England team – almost 100 players have come and gone – has managed just 56 hundreds of its own. Tendulkar has all but matched an entire major cricketing nation.

This is a level of greatness you feel bound to stroll around, to frown at, and perhaps even reverently buy a postcard of. It is unarguably, legally enforceably great, its greatness beyond quibble and reservation. But still, something seems to nag. Preferring Tendulkar to, say, the visceral, occasionally ragged genius of Brian Lara, or the Paul-Newman-riding a-bike-around-a-haystack romance of VVS Laxman seemed to go against some basic instinct, like preferring Luke Skywalker to Han Solo, or claiming that Jesus, not the devil, always has the best tunes.

The run machine has a human face, albeit one with handsome crow's feet, a few grey hairs and a cheeky grin

We have throughout his career heard a lot of talk about Tendulkar's grace in carrying the hopes of a billion countrymen. Undeniably this is admirable, but still you yearned quietly for some sign of rebellion, for a show of deliciously indulgent selfishness. Perhaps for a Virender Sehwag-style six-and-out on the first morning of a Test Match, a world-weary session of slog and waft, or even just some sense of unbending selfishness behind the unerringly cool head prefect demeanour.

For a while this made him strangely unsympathetic to the non-partisan. I can even remember laughing horribly, perhaps even punching the air, as England successfully perpetrated its most shameful anti-Tendulkar ruse on the 2001 tour of India. During the third Test in Bangalore the English skipper Nasser Hussain instructed his dreadfully uninspiring left-arm spinner Ashley Giles to bowl persistently and well wide of Tendulkar's leg stump, a tactic of utter negativity designed to bore the master batsman out.

This carried on for over after over. It wasn't pretty. Instead it was a deeply destructive, roundhead response to the proximity of greatness. It worked though. Eventually Tendulkar's circuits jammed, he leapt outside his leg stump to attack the bowling and was stumped. Gracious as ever, he simply walked off, while back home via satellite a nation crowed.

This was the way it was, not just for me, but many cricket fans beyond the subcontinent, those of us reared on the smouldering, occasionally brutal brilliance of the great West Indians, or the gnarliness of Steve Waugh's Aussies. We got Tendulkar. But we didn't wholly get him. The genius was clear, but it was a solemn genius, a churchy and refined genius.

Anyway, that's all gone out of the window now. I take it all back. Let me take this moment to officially draw a veil over all of this. I confess to these guilty feelings only because something very fundamental— and your favourite Test cricketer is one of the most fundamental things there is has shifted. I think it has to do with changing times, the slow revelation of character, and above all to do with age: his rather than mine. Tendulkar is approaching 40 but he simply will not weaken or fray at the edges. This is now clearly something far more than simply high-spec excellence.

Tendulkar is Test cricket's enduring guardian, its unanswerable stamp of approval

For the dithering unbeliever that last vital sense of wild and alluring extremity has come with the recklessness of Tendulkar's longevity, this most un-mechanical, un-robotic refusal to wither. It's the Rolling Stones principle in miniature: mildly embarrassing on stage aged 47; deeply rock and roll on stage aged 67. Tendulkar endures, his magnificence made human by the chastening dedication of his late years. Plus there has been a mellowing to the man himself. He smiles a lot more now. The beautifully supple wrists, the small decisive, millimetre perfect movement are all still in place. But this now a rather grizzled, charmingly sober and humble old dude of a master-batsman. The run machine has human face, albeit one with handsome crow's feet, a few grey hairs and a cheeky grin.

In saying all this, it is hard not to feel now like just another supplicant, one more convert in a wailing sea of Tendulkar-zealots. Here we have yet another person who believes that the Beatles are a good band, that Coca Cola is a refreshing drink and jeans are a comfortable type of trouser.

It turns out, however, that this isn't the case. Tendulkar is a generous icon. He inspires, I have discovered, a very personal kind of reverence. It is a broad church and we can all find our own personal experience of pure Sachin within it.

For what it's worth my own revelation of Tendulkar-ness was sealed with the realisation that he has, finally, entered my range of personal air cricket shots. This is no small matter. Air cricket is much more than just the most widely practised shadow-sport in the world. It is also a hugely intimate affair. If the game is in your blood this is something you will recognise as more than simply an idle pass-time for the work-shy or the bored. It is instead a fundamental expression of something far more fundamental. Or, at least, something – fundamentally – along these fundamental lines.

First an explanation for the novice. Air cricket is cricket you play only in mime form, often using a bat-like object, and perhaps making a 'clonk' noise as you despatch an imaginary ball from your presence. Over time it can become an almost Tai Chi-like practice, exercise not just for the muscles and tendons, but for the imagination too.

It is a universal practice too. I raised the subject of air cricket on *The Guardian* newspaper's over-by-over Test Match internet commentary recently and was swamped with stories in response: The man who performed an air cricket lofted drive with his rolled degree certificate at his graduation and sent it sailing into the audience; the Russian wedding almost ruined by a display of aggressive umbrella air-batsmanship; the hospital ward practice of playing air cricket with a drip stand. And all those men out there who have carried superfluous umbrellas for years, or kept cardboard tubes or walking sticks or old squash rackets about the house purely to facilitate their air cricket.

It is an instinctive business: I have a friend who finds himself automatically playing a perfect straight bat air-defensive shot on entering any crowded room. My own repertoire contains an increasingly instinctive recurrent air-leave, a Kevin Pietersen style disdainful waft of the bat into the air above stump level, which I find myself performing automatically whenever I'm caught up in a particularly long and boring non-essential conversation.

This instinctive quality is the clincher where Tendulkar is concerned. It turns out you can only ever really play air cricket shots that have "belonged" to cricketers you have loved. I still have a pirouetting Alec Stewart air-pull. I have a backside-waggling Graham Gooch clip through midwicket, and even a left-handed Sanath Jayasuriya mow over cover (always from the first ball of a 50-over run chase, the ball sent skimming into the stands for a brute-strength six).

Plus, brilliantly, I now have an air Tendulkar. This is my own revelation of the late, enduring, only slightly grizzled Tendulkar. It is a signature shot too, the wristy flick to leg for a strike-rotating single. A sway into line followed by a rotation of the hands. Occasionally, I alternate this with the similar, but more zingingly well-timed punch-block drive to the midwicket boundary. Hand me an umbrella. Give me a wooden spoon. This is what you'll get now. It might not seem like much, in the grand scheme of things. But I have no higher form of praise.

There is a final point about Tendulkar. Air cricket is, as a rule, Test cricket. It speaks mainly to the longer form of the game with its more balanced, balletic and technically refined movements. This is fitting because Tendulkar is above all a Test cricketer. It might even seem paradoxical that India's premier cricketer – the main man in a country where the joyful thrash of Twenty20 cricket is being furiously distilled as the coming force—doesn't even play in Twenty20 internationals.

It is also a wonderful thing. Tendulkar is Test cricket's enduring guardian, its unanswerable stamp of approval. He is in his small way the sentry at the gates beating back the barbarians, cricket's greatest populist lending his weight to its most rarefied form. Along with Ricky Ponting, he is also the last great Test player of this generation, the final generation to be raised in an era when the longer game was unarguably the main show. Perhaps with Tendulkar it might even, over time, turn out to be a case of saving the very best until the very last.

BARNEY RONAY is a senior sports writer of The Guardian.

187
SAHARA

ADOPTING SACHIN

Mike Coward

That Indo-Australian cricket has attained a heady status is largely due to Tendulkar's greatness

This pleasurable exercise requires an admission at the start. If the impartiality I hold dear is ever questioned it will be because of Sachin Ramesh Tendulkar.

Confession: It is true that I cannot access my digital diary and at least one bank account without entering 'Sachin' or 'Tendulkar' when prompted for a password or security code. This is evidence enough that even a journalist vigorously schooled to be totally objective can have a player at the forefront of his mind and secretly thrill to his brilliance.

As it is, I don't much like the notion of 'total objectivity' which smacks of remoteness and emotional detachment. And without exception the best writing is always accessible and passionate. Fairness and honesty should be the objective.

The reach of the Indian diaspora notwithstanding, Australians, it must be said, are often mystified by India and Indians. Perhaps this is a corollary of the geographical and cultural isolation of the poet's sunburnt country of sweeping plains and ragged mountain ranges. But surely we should leave this discussion to the social scientists and anthropologists.

Often the saving grace and a merciful ice-breaker is the shared enjoyment of cricket. This, at least, is a common language although this does not always make for the easiest conversation as we saw in Sydney in 2008 following the awful contretemps between Harbhajan Singh and Andrew Symonds.

Juxtapose this boorishness with the graciousness in play when Don Bradman scored his 100th first-class hundred while captaining an Australian XI against Lala Amarnath's Indian visitors also in Sydney 60 years earlier.

It is a rich part of the lore of the game that Gogumal Kishenchand, a very occasional leg-spinner employed by Lala Amarnath on the spur of the moment for the last over before the tea adjournment, took enormous pride in being the player off whom Bradman scored the precious run he needed to complete his triumph. Such was the Indian team's adulation of Bradman.

Sachin Tendulkar as popular screen villian 'Gabbar Singh' during a team-building exercise.

When film of the moment was shown in England, the renowned cricket writer, R. C. Robertson-Glasgow famously observed: "At the historic statistical moment, when Bradman was about to go from 99 to 100, there was the Indian bowler trying to deliver the ball with one hand and applaud with the other, a feat that is beyond the most enthusiastic practitioner."

While it is true this was also the match in which Vinoo Mankad ran out Bill Brown at the bowler's end so giving rise to the contentious 'Mankaded' dismissal, it was the deference of the Indian cricketer on this and subsequent visits that was so conspicuous to Australian watchers . .

Just occasionally, the Australian people will take an overseas player to their heart and claim him as their own

And perhaps because of this perceived acquiescence along with the paucity of visits in the 1960s and 1970s there was very little emotional engagement with Indian teams. Indeed, these matches were considered little more than a periodic addendum to Ashes and Frank Worrell Trophy cricket. It was not until the 1980s when Allan Border demanded Australian cricket stop the ugly and wholly unacceptable aping of England's culturally elitist view of Indian cricket that Indo-Australian cricket assumed its rightful importance. And no sooner had Australian cricket and its community become more aware and worldly than the game's devotees effectively prostrated themselves before a living deity in the Indian pantheon and happily adopted Tendulkar.

Just occasionally, the Australian people will take an overseas player to their heart and claim him as their own. But perhaps not since David Gower at 21 in 1978 has the embrace of a foreign player been so vigorous, so sustained.

Indeed, all the emotional standing ovations of farewell afforded him around the country in 2007-08 may now have to be reprised in 2011-12. Not even the inevitable upheavals of mid-life and the toll of more than 20 years in the rarefied atmosphere of the international arena has wearied him. He is indefatigable; seemingly unconquerable; unique.

In a European context, Australia is a young country and it has always looked to its young and ambitious. It has never been afraid of the rawness, arrogance and naked ambition of youth. Generally it is inspired by it and celebrates it in business, politics and sport; in every way.

Certainly, this in part explains the depth of the relationship between the Australian people and Tendulkar. When he was first in Australia he was just six months past his 18th birthday and while Australian cricket folk had pitifully little knowledge of cricket on the Indian sub-continent word had somehow filtered through of his derring-do as a 16-year-old against Wasim Akram and Waqar Younis in Pakistan.

Undeniably there was a sense of anticipation and he promptly confirmed his potential for greatness with head-turning hundreds in the disparate conditions to be found in Sydney and Perth. Soon enough he was anointed the *Little Master* and when he returned as his country's captain eight years later it was to the ultimate endorsement from *The Master,* Don Bradman.

The story goes that Bradman, at his home in the leafy eastern Adelaide suburb of Kensington Park, called to his wife Lady Jessie to come to the television and watch Tendulkar at the crease. In a rare television interview in 1996, Bradman told his interviewer: "I asked my wife to come and look at him. Now I never saw myself play, but I feel that this fellow is playing much the same as I used to play." She looked at him and said, "Yes, there is a similarity between the two."

"I can't explain in detail. To me it's his compactness, his technique, his stroke production, it all seemed to gel as far as I was concerned. That was how I felt." And bear in mind that Lady Jessie was the only person in the world who could question or contradict the Don. And she didn't on this occasion.

Tendulkar was flattered and embarrassed in equal measure by the comparison which was widely reported wherever the game is played. Neil Harvey, who rarely speaks well of the contemporary cricketer, agreed with Bradman but former England all-rounder Trevor Bailey considered Tendulkar to be the more orthodox.

Tendulkar was flattered and embarrassed in equal measure by the comparison

Soon enough the story was enshrined in the lore of the game and it was fitting that Tendulkar travelled to Australia to be the chief guest at a lavish function to celebrate Bradman's 90th birthday in 1998. And while Bradman was not physically strong enough to attend the dinner he did receive Tendulkar at his home where they shared their deep love for the game. There was, therefore, deep sadness 30 months later when Tendulkar was at home in Mumbai and preparing for a Test match with Australia at the Wankhede Stadium when Bradman died in Adelaide at 92. Indeed, one sensed some surprise at his passing for there had long been an expectation his century was inevitable. At worst, he would have made 99.94.

The poignancy was greater for Tendulkar as the night before the dark morning which brought the news he had hung a treasured photograph in the music room of his home in the northern suburb of Bandra West. It was the image of himself with Bradman taken that unforgettable August afternoon in the family room facing Holden Street at Kensington Park – a room which contained his beloved Brinsmead grand piano and, in that sense, doubled as his music room.

I have had the good fortune to know and interview both men and certainly recognise that from the earliest age each was inspired and sustained by music. Furthermore, as prisoners of fame, their music rooms provided a favoured and most welcome sanctuary.

Tendulkar was named by his brothers Nitin and Ajit and sister Savita after popular Bengali folk singer Sachin Dev Burman and as a child Bradman was taught the piano by his sister Lillian, who was destined to become a professional piano teacher. But truth be told he didn't need much help from his sibling. He was as natural at the keyboard as he was at the crease.

While Tendulkar has always jealously guarded the detail of his precious conversation with Bradman, it is fair to surmise that there would have been more pressing matters than sharing his love of the music of Mark Knopfler, The Eagles, Bob Marley, Queen and Pink Floyd along with special Indian songs. And Bradman no doubt resisted the urge to talk of the joys of Mozart or his song *Every Day is a Rainbow Day for Me,* which he wrote soon after his seminal tour of England in 1930.

The love of music and a penchant for playing off the back foot especially in front of square leg was not all they shared. Similar in stature – Tendulkar standing at 5ft 4in, 2¾in shorter than Bradman – each placed great store in the importance of family and the need for common decency and humility. And there can be little doubt that each had a clear idea of his place in history while he was making it.

Living with the heavy burden of celebrity may well have occupied some of their time as each was compelled to live life in the public gaze. Indeed, as he grew older Bradman became increasingly resistant to any intrusion into his private life and railed against the impertinence of the forever burgeoning and demanding media. To this end it will be fascinating to observe Tendulkar when he leaves the game with records that cannot conceivably be broken. It could be that he will forever be a prisoner of his fame.

Following his visit to Bradman's home, Tendulkar accompanied his friend Shane Warne on a wander through the Rundle Mall which dissects the main shopping precinct in the heart of Adelaide. Arguably the world's two most identifiable cricketers were readily recognised and engaged in casual conversation but they were neither mobbed nor inconvenienced and Tendulkar confided to Warne how he envied him the freedom to go where and when he pleased.

That Indo-Australian cricket has attained a heady status is largely due to Tendulkar's greatness as a player. There have been 28 Test matches since the Border-Gavaskar Trophy was instituted in 1996 with India winning 12 and Australia eight. Tendulkar, Rahul Dravid and Australian captain Ricky Ponting are the only survivors of the inaugural encounter for the Trophy at the Feroz Shah Kotla ground.

Australian cricket lovers' affection for Tendulkar has become more apparent with his every visit and the scenes of emotion in 2007-08, in the belief that he was on his farewell tour, were remarkable for their unselfconsciousness. When asked if it was indeed his last visit he simply smiled that familiar, gentle and endearing smile as if to say "do you seriously think it would be beyond me to return?" Of course, nothing seems beyond him for we have never seen his like.

Australians have marvelled he has never been bowed by the enormous burden of carrying the hopes of millions, are fascinated by tales, many apocryphal, of his disguises in public places and of his high speed thrill drives to Pune and scarcely conceal their amusement at him being a member of the Middle Income Group Club (MIGC) in Bandra East.

Growing up in Adelaide my summer God was Les Favell and life was not quite the same when he retired. And something within me could not be replaced when he died of kidney cancer at the age of 57 in 1987. Through the newspaper industry I got to know Les and he was every bit the hero I imagined him to be as a boy.

I watch Tendulkar as I watched Les. I can pay him no greater compliment than that. And in our many professional dealings he has always been approachable, affable and respectful; a true gentlemen. And I know that when he finishes, life will again not quite be the same. But until then I will, along with many others, be sustained by the thought that the little bloke, as Bradman was also called, will return one more time to the great southern land and to those who are happy to adopt him.

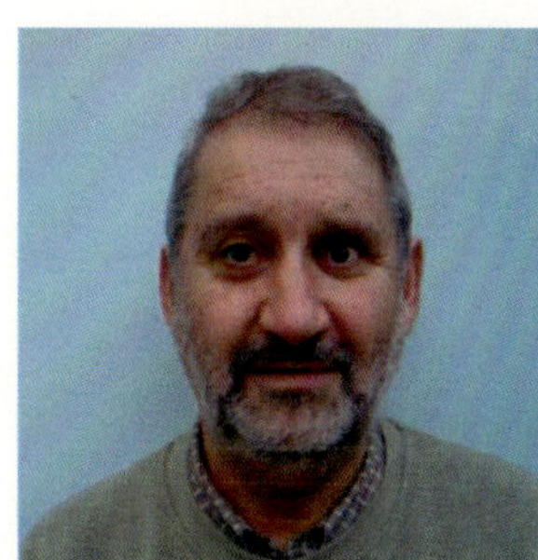

MIKE COWARD's Cricket Beyond The Bazaar *explores Indo-Australian cricketing traditions.*

Another wicket, another celebration: Rahul Dravid helps celebrate Pragyan Ojha's wicket.

SAHARA
187
SAHA
SAHARA

SMART COACHING

Sanjay Manjrekar

I shudder to think what today's coaches would have done with Tendulkar

There is no doubt in my mind that Sachin Tendulkar was a child prodigy. But to attribute all his success to god-given talent would be unfair to Tendulkar first, and then to his coach, Ramakant Achrekar. For Tendulkar worked bloody hard on his skills and that along with his natural talent is what has made him the greatest run machine of all time.

When I say worked hard, it really wasn't work at all for a 12-year-old, was it? Tendulkar was just having fun, playing cricket. A game that he loved to play (not follow or read about. Up and coming cricketers are rarely interested in reading about or watching cricket. They only like playing it). And thank God there was Achrekar around for Tendulkar. I shudder to think what today's coaches, obsessed with the mechanics of cricket and intent on complicating a simple game, would have done with Tendulkar.

The first and obvious thing they would have done is change his unorthodox batting grip and sent him on the path to mediocrity. So here was a coming together of two simple people, Achrekar and Tendulkar, to give us a phenomenal passage in the history of the game.

Tendulkar obviously is special but Achrekar was not. Not by any stretch of the imagination, and not in the sense that would automatically make him one of the great coaches in the game.

Achrekar did nothing different with Tendulkar. He just applied his same trusted formula as he did to the hundreds of other promising Mumbai cricketers under him. And the formula was quite simple. Want to be a good cricketer? Well, then go and play lots of cricket.

Malcolm Gladwell has written in *Outliers*, his study of what makes people exceptional, about the 'ten thousand hour rule'. Those who make it to the top he says work harder, *much* harder than anyone else. "Excellence," he says, "requires a critical minimum level of practice." Gladwell settles on ten thousand hours as the magic number for true expertise. You can argue over the figure, but

With Sanjay Manjrekar on Sachin's debut series in Pakistan.

the principle is sound. And Tendulkar played more cricket at a higher level than any of his contemporaries. His idea of relaxation was to play more cricket.

And play he did, for hours and days and weeks and months, oblivious to most other things. Tendulkar made his debut for Mumbai in the Ranji Trophy at the age of 14. Now 14 is obviously a very tender age to be playing first class cricket. And he was a genuine 14-year-old, not one of those 14-year-olds popular in our age-group tournaments who shaved clean every morning to look 14.

Tendulkar at 14 had played more cricket matches than I had at the age of 19 (when I made my first class debut). So here is another case in point for Gladwell's theory on genius. By that age, Tendulkar was already battle hardened and ready to take on the big boys with the approach and attitude of a 20-year-old.

He had strong legs and strong forearms too and that was by playing countless numbers of Achrekar's friendly matches and attending the relentless net sessions. Tendulkar also used a very heavy bat, one of the heaviest used at that time. So batting with it constantly was like the frequent gym sessions that modern players go through to strengthen their forearms.

With two important differences, though. Tendulkar's batting was getting better all the time and what's more, he was having fun doing the 'weight training'. Achrekar was a big believer in

The Mumbai pair, now older and wiser.

match practice. So on days when his boys did not have any official junior matches he would get them to play friendly matches amongst themselves.

And there were net sessions before and after the game. Achrekar did just one thing differently for his exceptionally gifted boys like Tendulkar. He gave them extra net sessions. Which meant at the Shivaji Park Maidan, where there would be at least 15 net sessions going on simultaneously, Achrekar would use his clout to get Tendulkar to bat in four nets. One after the other.

Achrekar had just one net session that was his own, but the guys who ran the other nets obliged him. This is one of the secrets of Mumbai's success and the reason they keep producing quality players. Exceptional talent excites the Mumbai cricket community. Hence Tendulkar the 'outsider' was more than welcome at those other nets.

He was having fun doing the 'weight training'

It is because of this Mumbai trait that we senior Mumbai players playing for India had already heard about Sachin Tendulkar and Vinod Kambli even before they had played grade A cricket in Mumbai. "Watch out for these two new Achrekar boys" we were told. Because the Achrekar boys played so many matches they were generally good at all aspects of the game.

Fielding, catching, running between the wickets, especially, can only be significantly improved by playing more matches. Also the one vital characteristic that separates the best from the good is what is called 'street smartness'.

Another term for the same is match fitness, the little things that you latch onto to win matches and have an edge over the opposition. This was an important by-product of Achrekar's theory of playing more and more matches. I have failed to understand why today's coaches don't take a good look at how Sachin Tendulkar became 'Sachin Tendulkar'. All they need to do then is duplicate his training methods and they would be able to create, maybe not more Tendulkars, but certainly some very outstanding batsmen.

Tendulkar as a little boy was also cheeky and naughty. It is said that this was one important reason his brother Ajit pushed him early into sports - to keep him away from mischief and to channelise all that energy.

So, being naughty and cheeky became advantages in this competitive team sport. Cricket is not for the 'nerds' is it? It is meant for those talented, cheeky little competitive kids. The 'nerds' can run the sport though. Of course not every one of Achrekar's boys became a Tendulkar. That is because of what Sachin brought to the table himself. The unparalleled will to succeed. That deep, strong resolve that cannot be seen on the outside: To be the best and settle for nothing less.

He beat an accomplished state table tennis player while we were playing a Ranji Trophy game in Gujarat in a sports complex. Tendulkar loves ball games and when he got bored just sitting around in the dressing room he wandered into the table tennis section of the complex. It was here that he got into a duel with the state table tennis player. A small crowd gathered. Now Tendulkar was not going to lose at any cost. He was in the public domain which meant he could not come second best, even if the guy was better trained than him.

Tendulkar hates failures like no one else does

But the guy could not have anticipated the tremendous will to win of Tendulkar and that is where he lost out. I have always secretly felt that Tendulkar would have been even more successful a sportsman had he chosen an individual sport.

I would like to believe that if there was any other individual sport as popular as cricket in India, Tendulkar may have pursued that and become a star at it. He is lucky that he was born with prodigious talent, if not he would have been quite a frustrated cricketer. Because I cannot imagine Tendulkar being content being just another good cricketer.

We all hate failures but Tendulkar hates failures like no one else does. It was this trait that I had talked about in that period of his career when I thought that Tendulkar was getting a bit too obsessed with trying not to fail rather than going out to succeed.

I remember a festival match at Eden Gardens, Kolkata, when he got out very early in the innings. He was surprised the umpire did not call a 'no ball' (as they did in fun games) when the ball was in the air descending towards long off. The fielder made the catch. Tendulkar stood his ground and refused to walk off. He badly wanted to bat on.

The umpire, who had already turned a deep purple at not having called a no ball had no choice but to raise his finger. A crowd of some 70,000 people saw Tendulkar hit the ball down the throat of long off and could not understand why he was still waiting and refusing to leave the field.

We the players in the opposition, just to tease him, protested and gestured exaggeratedly so the crowd would think we were very unhappy with the situation. By now Tendulkar also was turning purple but he stayed on. Under his breath he kept pleading to us to let him bat on. Its only a fun game ...

Well, we relented and Tendulkar continued to bat on. The crowd was confused for a while after what they had seen. But they soon recovered and settled back in their seats to enjoy the Tendulkar show.

I know now that a very similar incident took place a few years back in Australia and that too, would you believe it, in an official international match when the batsman refused to walk off after being caught in the deep.

The batsman? One Mr Greg Chappell. Go figure...

At this stage of Sachin's career if I have to give just one reason for his success, even in the 21st year of his international career it has to be the sheer, almost desperate will to succeed.

SANJAY MANJREKAR is a commentator who played alongside Tendulkar for Mumbai and India in the 1990s.

ABOVE HYPE

Makarand Waingankar

Those who know him well believe that he has a few thousand runs more in his kitty

Mumbai, the fast-paced, adrenaline-charged city that never sleeps, ironically supports a game that moves at a gentle pace enchanting and entertaining at the same time. The passion is evident in every by-lane where children play cricket for want of grounds and facilities. Fans, old and young, eagerly await the newspaper and turn immediately to the sports page to discuss, dissect and speculate.

It's not uncommon to see a ten-year-old with a schoolbag on his back and a cricket bat in his hand, at the bus stand or railway platform, playing air-cricket shots in imitation of his heroes. He is prepared for flak for not doing his homework but he will seldom miss match practice. It's the child's first infatuation that grows into a life-long love epic.

In the early 1980s one such kid from the New English School in Bandra, burdened with homework requested his parents to change his school. The reason - the school didn't participate in inter-schools cricket tournament. This 12-year old kid then joined the Shardashram Vidyamandir High School at Shivaji Park that produced the likes of Vinod Kambli who averages over 50 in Test matches, Amol Muzumdar, highest run-getter of national championship of India and Pravin Amre who scored a century on his debut against South Africa.

In October of that year I got a request from his coach to include him in one of the four teams for the under-19 selection trial tournament that I was conducting. Frankly speaking, I felt the coach was being overconfident of the boy's abilities as there was nothing to suggest from his small frame that he fit into senior company.

A 12-year old in an under-19 tournament? One selector agreed, and that was enough. The expressions on the faces of the players in his team said it all. Their eyes were questioning the audacity of the selectors to push a kid through the back door.

The kid didn't get to bat but so determined he was that he had padded up much before the openers did though he was to bat down the order. He was very keen to be in the middle. And perhaps wondering why the openers weren't padding up quickly.

In the next match he hit a century with some brilliant shots. Sachin Ramesh Tendulkar - the cricketer had well and truly arrived in 1985. He was picked only for the under-15 Mumbai team though he had excelled in the under-19 selection matches!

Despite the fact that he whipped the bowlers who were so much older to him, the selectors felt he was too young to play under 19 cricket. Four years later he was playing for the country against Pakistan!

The legendary Gundappa Vishwanath had a similar problem in his time. He was turned away from the state's junior selection trials because of his diminutive frame. He went on to play 91 Tests.

That season Sachin amassed more than 2500 runs for the school and the state but when he wasn't chosen for the Mumbai Cricket Association's Best Junior Cricketer award, he wept bitterly. Sunil Gavaskar sent him a hand written letter saying 'yours truly and Dilip Vengsarkar too weren't chosen for that award and both of us didn't do too badly in international cricket...'

He had padded up
much before the openers
though he was to bat down the order

In the under 15 inter-state tournament, he scored 123 in no time against Baroda. There is a story that coach Tukaram Surve (opening partner of India captain Nari Contractor for Gujarat) doesn't tire of narrating.

The team reached Ahmedabad railway station in the early hours. No sooner did they reach the club where they were staying, than the kids climbed into their beds to catch the remainder of their sleep. As Surve went around for a headcount, he found the youngest player Sachin missing. He pressed the panic button and alerted the manager. Both rushed to the security at the main gate who confirmed that no one had left the premises.

Soon they heard a sound of something hitting the wall. They followed the sound that took them to the terrace. Needless to say, they found Sachin throwing the ball on the wall and getting ready to play copybook shots.

He refused to return to his room. When the match began, his enthusiasm and involvement according to Surve was such that he was asked to field at third man. But his start from third man would end near point!

In the year that he played the under-19 selection matches, he was playing a senior tournament for the MIG Cricket club. The non-striker remembers a ball going past Sachin's right eye. Satish Samant the senior pro walked down and said "You were lucky. Your right eye would have gone with

the ball." The tiny fellow replied, "but had I connected, it would have gone for a six." The next ball he sent soaring out of the ground and followed that with four shots to the boundary.

In that famous 664-run partnership with Vinod Kambli, the captain of the opposing team, St. Xavier's, Sairaj Bahutule, says the way Sachin and Vinod were hitting on the open maidan, his players were getting fatigued from retrieving the ball, so long were the hits. After fielding for two days, some of the boys asked the captain to concede the game because they had no energy left to field any more. One bowler refused to complete the over.

The following day in the junior match against the Anjuman-i-Islam which was known to play overage players, the Anjuman boys scored 380 with the support of huge crowd support from their school. Sachin's school had lost 3 wickets for 30 and in walked Amol Muzumdar who in the previous match had been padded up till teatime of the second day.

Amol tried to play a drive and was fortunate that ball went in between the slip fielders. Sachin walked down the wicket and told him in no uncertain terms "Amol if you play like this, we will be four down and won't be able to win the game. Put your head down. We scored 800 a few days back. We just can't afford to lose" With both getting unbeaten hundreds, Sachin's Shardashram school won the game by seven wickets.

Shardashram was a small school that was not known for its academics. Cricket seemed to be the school's claim to fame. Sachin was in the morning school. The classes would begin at seven in the morning but Sachin's gang of cricketers would be in the school at 6.30 to play underhand tennis ball cricket.

Right behind the playing area was the kitchen of one of the residents of that chawl. In one game, Sachin hit the ball so hard that the utensils in the kitchen came tumbling down. The boys ran to their classrooms and went about their routine. During assembly there was an announcement on the PA system summoning the boys who had been playing cricket to come forward. And when they did, they received a fair share of spanking and were sent back home.

Not to be outdone by the small problem of having to explain the scenario to parents, Sachin came up with a solution. They went to the nearby Shivaji Park beach and played cricket in the school hours and then ambled on to join coach Achrekar at the nets at the Shivaji Park maidan.

"We scored 800 a few days back.
We just can't afford to lose"

Former Mumbai captain Nilesh Kulkarni remembers Sachin going for practice when the Indian team had already practised for four hours. When Nilesh met him in the foyer of the hotel, he was going for practice again. "Where are you headed", Nilesh asked. To which he replied "I will be going for the captain's meeting tomorrow so I thought of having a good knock today because I will be missing practice tomorrow !"

There are hundreds of anecdotes from his early days that foretell the inevitable greatness. Once in a school match he kept hitting so many balls out of the ground that the opposition had to borrow balls from Sachin's school.

That he scored a hundred on his first class debut is a known fact but to him it was another school match. Only a couple of days earlier he had played a school match and scored a big hundred. He was not overawed by the presence of seniors like Vengsarkar who had played for the country for more than a decade. The confidence was that of a player who is above hype. Neither smug nor insecure.

Sachin wasn't happy with the 20-minute batting stints he was getting in the Ranji nets. After practice he would chase one of the senior bowlers, Kiran Mokashi, to bowl to him. It is said that one ingredient that separates the great from the good is the ability to compete with oneself. Tendulkar has never rested on his laurels. He has been known to overdo the practice trying to perfect his style and work on his flaws until they dissolve.

Sachin hasn't changed at all despite success and rise in stardom. His work ethic is the same. Now he practices at the Mumbai Cricket Association's cricket academy with an eye on perfection and time management. His practice process is planned meticulously. Training, fielding, running and batting are all done with a strategic goal.

There was a time four years ago when he was getting frustrated with a particularly nasty tennis elbow. Not being able to touch a bat was the biggest punishment for him but he successfully emerged out of this difficult phase by remaining focussed and positive.

The remarkable quality which cricket buffs who mull over the technicalities of the skill have observed, is that he had made his game a bit tighter. Expansive drives thumped to boundary are fewer than those he caresses which bisect the fielders. That's the art he has developed. Great control and economy of movement in the crease are his trademark.

A decade ago the bat was only used to whip the ball; now the real art of batsmanship is on display. As Muzumdar says, the maturity was there at 17 and 20 years later it is still there but what is evident is the goal that he sets for the game. Apart from the lofty ideal of playing for the country and winning the game, he has the individual drive for perfection and beauty.

What would he do after he announces his retirement is a million dollar question. I doubt he is even thinking about it. Those who know him well believe that he has a few thousand runs more in his kitty.

The most worshipped cricketer of his time, he doesn't let the cult status that fans have accorded, impact his demeanour. Watching the reigning 'God' at his best is almost a religious experience for the fans. It's not a sport, a game or a life-long passion, it's sublime devotion.

MAKARAND WAINGANKAR is a coach and columnist from Mumbai.

BOWLER'S DELIGHT

Anil Kumble

At his best, he impressed upon the bowler the sheer futility of having any fielders at all

Sachin and I once scored centuries on the same day. It was an under-17 tournament, and in different matches, and for different teams, but by then he was already the best known schoolboy cricketer in the world. The vagaries of the Indian domestic cricket are such that I never got to bowl to him in the national championship which is strange when you consider that I played nearly two decades of first class cricket, and he continues to play despite having made his debut earlier.

I am often asked how I would have bowled to him (we have played against each other in other matches). I think I would have bowled differently at different times in his career. In the early years, when a youthful Sachin delighted in taking you on at your own game, I would have packed the off side field and bowled outside the off stump. The young Sachin did not believe in playing the percentages; he was always determined to impose his will on the bowler. And his response would have been to pierce the off side field.

I have heard it said of Don Bradman that every time you moved a fielder, he showed you up by hitting the ball through the new gap that opened up. Sachin was more subtle. At his best, he impressed upon the bowler the sheer futility of having any fielders at all. He drove with such precision that he could drill the ball within inches of a fielder and get it past him before he had moved.

In later years, he might have simply taken advantage of the less populated onside and played in that direction. Were I to bowl to him then, I would mix it up more, challenging him to play across the line with the possibility of getting him leg before.

All wonderful in theory, of course, but Sachin was fully capable of turning theories on their head. And finding opportunities to score where none existed just before he had made it look not

The great batsman watches the great bowler at the nets.

just possible, but inevitable. That is why I rate his 241 at Sydney so highly. He had been getting out trying to drive through cover, as sometimes happens to the best of batsmen, and so decided to simply eliminate that most productive of his strokes.

Batsmen sometimes add a stroke to their repertoire and make runs; here was a case of a supremely gifted batsman actually reducing his armoury and finishing more successful than before.

Such is his cricketing brain that I am convinced he would have been a great player even without his batting! I always envied his leg spin which he bowled with such control so naturally. He has not been given enough credit as a bowler who tried everything – medium pace, off spin, leg spin, off cutters, leg cutters – and understood bowling like few did. Perhaps this understanding of the bowler's craft enhanced his batsmanship as he seemed to be always aware of just what the bowler was thinking. Hence his legendary reputation as a batsman who could get the bowler to bowl where he, Sachin, wanted.

A man who likes to be in control.

Curiously enough, it wasn't the Wasim Akrams or the Shane Warnes who caused him trouble as a batsman, but Hansie Cronje and the New Zealander Dion Nash. Commentators might dismiss them as 'dibbly-dobbly' bowlers, but somehow Sachin enjoyed neither the dibble nor the dobble.

Neither did he seem to enjoy captaincy very much. This was partly because he expected everybody to be as involved as he was. He was criticised, in fact, for being over-involved. But that was a tribute to the wealth of ideas he always had, and he would share them with the enthusiasm of a child. Personally, as a bowler, I liked to be left alone to work things out, but I could understand his enthusiasm. Not many people realise that he led India in some tough series abroad – in fact he led more in away matches than at home – in Australia, in South Africa, Sri Lanka and the West Indies. Captaincy also meant that he had to deal with administrators who did not have either his vision or his experience or his intensity. When it wasn't working, he gave it up, and that was a mature thing to do at the time.

All that is so many years in the past now that a whole generation of players has come – and gone – while Tendulkar carries on merrily. That is the key word, for he is carrying on merrily, enjoying himself, enjoying the taking an ageing, tired and injury-ridden body through the challenges of the modern game. In his 'second coming', he has been even more creative than in his first, if such a thing is possible. There was an inevitability about him scoring one-day cricket's first-ever double century. What was not so inevitable was that he would do it at the age of 37, more than 20 years after he first hit Abdul Qadir for all those sixes in Pakistan to announce that he was ready for the shorter game. Amazingly, he prepares for a match the same way he did 20 years ago.

The young Sachin did not believe in playing the percentages

In the many years that I have known Sachin, he has not changed at all. He continues to be a family man, and today we discuss such things as the children's schooling! When he lets his hair down, he is a funny man, a mimic. When we toured together, he often displayed his passion for cars and his gift for identifying their makes while getting a glimpse of their roofs from within the team bus. He sat at the back then, which is rather like a newcomer fielding at short leg; now he takes his deserved place in front.

He continues to be a gadget freak, and prefers to listen to music on his headset to relax; he prefers to watch a match on television in the dressing room (I like to sit out and watch live). But in a strange way, despite our different backgrounds and the different paths we took to international cricket, we faced similar challenges. That of having to live up to expectations all the time. As a batsman he had to prove everybody right while as a bowler I had to prove everybody wrong!

We played over a hundred Test matches together, and somewhere along the line started a ritual that was much commented upon. Sachin, it must be mentioned, is not a particularly superstitious sort of a chap. He has had his share of bad decisions (especially from one umpire in particular), but he never looked outside of the game itself – as many players do – for reasons beyond the merely rational. No tantrums. No broken bats. He might occasionally shake his head to indicate discomfort with a decision, and that too while watching the replay in the dressing room. He might sit quietly for ten minutes or so. And then it would be back to normal.

But to get back to that superstitious ritual we shared. It happened during the Delhi Test against Pakistan when I had ten in an innings. Occasionally, as the tension grew, he would take my cap and hand it over to the umpire as I prepared to bowl. Each time he did that initially, a wicket fell. We saw this as an omen, and in later matches if the batsmen at the crease proved difficult to dislodge, he would run across from wherever he was fielding and hand my cap over if I was about to bowl. It worked sometimes. It didn't at other times. But it was fun to try.

More seriously, I relied on him for inputs especially if I was trying something new at the nets. It was a two-way street. Sachin had the humility to ask for comments when he was at the nets, or

indeed during a match. Was his foot coming across too much? Was he committing himself too early? Was his stance balanced? He liked to be constantly on top of these things.

In recent years, I have found him more relaxed, and more likely to let his hair down. He is the grey eminence of the side, and in his time India have won more Tests than they have lost which puts him and all those who played with him on a very high plane. Today he is like an indulgent elder in the family, allowing the youngsters to pull his leg, and often paying back in kind. He has a fund of stories, naturally, and the younger players are only too happy to gather around him as he holds forth. And his talent for mimicry has not deserted him (curiously enough, it is a gift that Sunil Gavaskar too possesses).

It wasn't the Akrams or the Warnes who troubled him, but Hansie Cronje and Dion Nash

He retains that intensity as a competitor that first marked him out as a teenager. He still hates to lose at table tennis, for example, a game he plays with a passion. He is not easily satisfied. If his body allows, I can see him play till he is over 40, because his mind is strong. Which means that he could still be breaking the hearts of bowlers for another five or six years if not more!

The best batsmen in my time have been Sachin, Brian Lara and Sri Lanka's Aravinda da Silva. But only one of them, Sachin, would be an automatic choice for an Earth XI versus Mars XI. Even if Mars somehow managed to attract Dion Nash to play for them!

It has been a privilege to be part of perhaps the finest Indian team of all time and play a role in taking it to the number one spot in the world. The pressure on Sachin the batsman has been reduced by the arrival of such greats as Rahul Dravid, V V S Laxman, Virender Sehwag and others. But the pressure of being Sachin is something else. Yet he has been a model as much off the field too, which is an achievement in itself.

ANIL KUMBLE, former captain, is India's highest wicket taker in international cricket and one of only two bowlers to claim all ten wickets in a Test innings.

A job well done, obviously— with Mahendra Singh Dhoni.

SAHARA
187

MARYADA PURUSHOTTAM

Bishan Bedi

I have dismissed him in an international match without even bowling to him!

Sachin Tendulkar's first Test captain, Krishnamachari Srikkanth is now Chairman of Selectors. Two other colleagues - Dilip Vengsarkar and Kiran More - have already completed their stints. His second captain, Mohammad Azharuddin is now a Member of Parliament as is another teammate, Navjot Sidhu.

Two others from his home town are well entrenched television commentators. Numerous others have just vanished from the scene. But SRT flows on serenely like an age-old river, giving no sign whatsoever of hanging up his boots.

I was the cricket manager on Sachin's first tour to England. That's when I observed the extraordinary glow on Sachin's face. My reaction in 1990 then was the kid is blessed with extraordinary talent. I'm not being wise now or saying "I told you so" but a strange feeling of spirituality is ever so gripping now. I don't look at SRT as just another human being, he is more than that. By his own admission he is aiming to go for another level of excellence. No living Indian sportsperson has ever expressed such an opinion. Mind you he is not talking of mastery or perfection of his craft. His vocabulary revolves around excellence. No one is perfect. Not even Sir Donald Bradman or Sir Garfield Sobers.

Ever since I met Sachin in 1990 I have tried to understand his psyche. For example why and how did he take up cricket and not any other sport? Cricket because of the Mumbai legacy perhaps? And batting more than any other aspect of the game. They say in England it is a social necessity (remember cricket is first and last an English sport), a class thing.

How did the English social necessity get into the very depths of a phenomenon called SRT? Perhaps some qualified psychologist may be able to work out an appropriate response. I'm not saying 'answer' because so much of SRT physically and mentally is not easily explained. What can be however is that SRT was not cut out for academic chores. The fact that he is so presentable has nothing to do with his education. Touring and playing cricket non-stop for more than two decades is an education in itself.

Besides, SRT is an excellent student of cricket. He needn't be one of science or maths. Perhaps one day when SRT retires and has empty moments like most of us do, maybe he'll miss the urge to lay his hands on a book and go through one like he is swallowing the bowlers from all opposition. But that is not for now. Indeed it is long time away.

Sometimes I feel, however, that it might have been a blessing that Sachin did not have to spend time with books while growing up. It meant he was completely focussed on the bat, to the exclusion of everything else.

I'm not too sure if he is familiar with Sir Neville Cardus. Cardus would have done justice to Sachin's profound cricket ability. If Cardus was the Tendulkar of cricket writing, Tendulkar is the Cardus of batsmanship. Pity the two lives never crossed. I was privileged to know both men. I've plenty of Cardus in my personal library. Can't say the same about SRT because I'm still studying him!

Sachin is a genius. Can anybody deny that? But we can always argue about how geniuses emerge. The most common phrase is that a "genius is born, not made" A lot of the credit for SRT's greatness belongs to his mother. Indeed, Sachin's parents have been a blessing not many present day kids can claim to have.

I think SRT owed it to the public to express himself on the burning issues of his time, like match-fixing and chucking

Sachin is a ship in a sea, a sea of commerce which he has negotiated without any mishap. Truly remarkable for someone who is a school dropout. Parental guidance is important here. In fact, right from his younger days, he has had a core group protecting him. Parents apart, there was his brother Ajit. Then later, his wife Anjali, a qualified doctor who chose not to practice but look after Sachin and the children instead.

In fact, even today in the dressing room, everyone looks after him. It is important for Indian cricket that Sachin retains his peace of mind in the dressing room. But there is more to it than that. There is something about him that invites the protective arm around the shoulder, the comforting word in the ear. I said after his first Test century at Old Trafford on that 1990 tour that women in England wanted to mother him; and those younger wanted to seduce him! I don't think much has changed in two decades.

"He reminds me of you," I told my Northants colleague Mushtaq Mohammed on that first tour, "but he will go much further and have a greater impact."

Mushtaq had made his debut at 15, and looked at home on the field in the company of grown men. Mushtaq's response was interesting, "If you have to make big scores, you have to start early.

Once you get into the 30s, it becomes difficult to bat for long. The experience will sap him."

Sachin may have left the big scores till too late. As his legion of fans point out, he does not have a century in each innings in a Test match, or a triple hundred, and too few doubles for a batsman of his class.

It is simplistic to compare Sachin and Bradman (in fact it has become a bit of a cliché), or Sachin and Lara, but I think the valid comparison is with Walter Hammond. The Englishman's record is quite incredible, and except briefly, he did not dominate the way Bradman did. Sachin has been consistent without dominating over long periods like Bradman or Viv Richards. He has invented shots that are uniquely his.

Colleagues were in awe of Hammond's consistency; colleagues are in awe of Sachin's. I once asked Bradman if he would have scored the same number of runs today, and he said, "No, Bish. But they won't get me out either. I'll adjust."

It is in this sense that Sachin is Bradman's equal. In the ability to adjust. To create new responses to new situations. He is probably superior to Hammond on that score. Of course, I have seen neither Bradman nor Hammond in action (except in old films), and I am going by statistics and responses alone.

In England 1990 with (from right) Kumble, Azharuddin, Hirwani and the physio.

The fact is that Sachin has loomed large in the minds of the two great modern bowlers – Glen McGrath and Shane Warne. And a whole generation of the best from all lands. It is an incredibly difficult thing to do, to carry a nation's batting on your shoulders for so long.

On their first England tour, I called Sachin and Sanjay Manjrekar aside and told them, "Boys, you must be aware that India's batting will rest on your shoulders for the next generation." Sanjay, who had made a brilliant century in the West Indies earlier and a double century in Pakistan, unfortunately did not last the course, although he had everything in abundance. Perhaps he tended to be distracted. I don't know.

But Sachin had no such problems. 'Distraction' is not a word that exists in his dictionary (if he has one!). Stories of his attending half a dozen nets as a schoolboy are legion.

There is something about him that invites the protective arm around the shoulder

From a very young age, Sachin understood the game. And I mean that in a profound sense. It wasn't just his batting. In the Lord's Test he took a running catch off Alan Lamb that was incredible for the manner he pulled it off and then threw the ball in the air in sheer, joyous abandonment. Beneath the action was the thinking of a man who knew where the ball would land and how to get there. His bowling gave the same sense of spatial awareness that great sportsmen possess but few think about.

I expected him to be one of the great captains. But he came up against opposition from some seniors, his predecessor Mohammad Azharuddin predominantly. There was a tour of the West Indies where Azhar was less than helpful (to put it mildly).

But just as Sachin will not take credit for anything he does or anything he is responsible for including his work for charity, he will not do the reverse either. He will not criticise those who were unhelpful. The comparison that comes to mind is with the Hindu deity Lord Ram, called 'Maryada Purushottam', or the ideal man, epitomising the highest discipline. When I say that, people say I am exaggerating and that it would be unfair to bestow god-like qualities on a mere human. But the whole point is that Sachin is not merely human!

He may or may not be conscious of being a 'Maryada Purushottam', but it has certainly kept him from speaking out his mind. It has meant that whatever he might think privately of his colleagues and their negative impact on the game, he will not go public with it. There was a case of a declaration against New Zealand in a Test match when Kapil Dev was the manager it would be interesting to know about.

Sachin Tendulkar shows the opposition how it can be done.

But that is not all. I think SRT owed it to the public to express himself on the burning issues of his time, like match-fixing and chucking. Both these ugly developments coincided with his time as the leading batsman of the world, and the grey eminence of his sport. But Sachin refused to be the spokesman for cricket or to express an opinion. He is intelligent enough to have one, but the public has not been taken into his confidence.

I can't imagine Bradman shirking this responsibility. The great Australian was part of cricket and its governing body for a little over half a century. In his time, the ICC was known as the Imperial Cricket Conference with the Indian Board having no say. Now the ICC cannot do without an Indian say. So SRT has a lot to do to catch up with Sir Donald on this score!

I suspect part of the reason for Sachin's ordinary record as captain was his lack of education – it might have enabled him to become a great batsman, but it stunted his growth as a great captain. Sachin had not grown beyond his region. He was happy only if he could converse in Marathi and had to have people around who could talk the same language. He grew into a world figure quite quickly, speaking in practised English and even picking up a few choice swear words in Punjabi (which has some of the choicest ones I can assure you!), but that came later.

Still, he was an excellent captain of Mumbai. I think the fact that he was leading a team where everyone spoke the same language made the difference.

I would have loved to bowl to Sachin. In fact, I have dismissed him in an international match without even bowling to him!

I was asked by both Shane Warne and Daniel Vettori when they were touring India about bowling to Sachin, and I told them both the same thing: bowl to get him out and not to contain him. Nobody can contain for long periods batsmen like Bradman, Sobers, Viv Richards, Brian Lara or Tendulkar.

But they are all fallible for one reason – ego. Bowlers can make the greatness of a great batsman work against him. Crowd them with close-in fielders and they will immediately like to show who is boss. On Warne's first trip to India, when Sachin became his nightmare, I told the bowler that a straight six was always hit off a good ball, and not to worry if the ball went over his head into the sightscreen. The best plan would be to have Sachin surrounded by close in fielders, especially at the start of his innings. "The ball keeps disappearing," Warne confessed!

Vettori too on his first tour of India had similar fears. We chatted at the Kotla. I told him I would make Sachin use his feet and prepare myself for a return catch. That's exactly what Vettori did, having Sachin caught and bowled off the third delivery he faced. And that's how I got SRT's wicket without bowling to him.

When bowling to the greats, Sobers, Barry Richards, Viv Richards, I have taken my share of stick. I don't think I'd have been over-awed by the prospect of getting mauled by Sachin. It would have been a privilege, and I would have enjoyed it.

Only the truly great batsman can make even those bowling to him look forward to the response. I once overheard Lindsay Hassett telling Arthur Morris that Bradman would have "murdered Bishan." But I would still have bowled an attacking line to him. As I would to Sachin Tendulkar.

BISHAN BEDI, manager on Sachin's first tour of England is a former India captain and one of the greatest spinners to have played the game.

SIMPLE MANTRA

Rahul Dravid

Like most great batsmen, Sachin has the ability to control where the bowlers bowl to him

I have heard it said of a former great – I think it was Len Hutton – that behind his mask was another mask. Sachin Tendulkar's case is just the opposite. Behind his simplicity is a genuine simplicity that only the truly great have in any field.

I first saw him when we were 14 in an age-group match in Cuttack. I was a substitute for South Zone, Sachin played for West and made some 60 runs. A year later we faced each other in Nagpur. I was struck by his talent, and his heavy bat, a Slazenger that many of us envied. A year later he was playing for India, facing Imran and Wasim Akram and Waqar Younis, while the rest of us were yet to play Ranji Trophy.

His early success as an India player gave state teams around the country the confidence to push teenagers into first class cricket. If earlier you had to wait till you were 19 or 20, now 17-year-olds were being given their chance. Both Sourav Ganguly and I made our debuts at 17. Vinod Kambli too made it to the national side early.

Sachin came into international cricket a finished product; by the age of 16 he had hit more cricket balls than I had at 25. Although we were the same age, he was senior to me in the Indian team by seven years, and was captain in my third Test match. All this defined my relationship with Sachin just as much as our similarities and differences as cricketers did. It meant that I looked up to him and was never in competition with him. We have played more than 125 Test matches together, and countless one-day internationals.

But as the years wore on and some of us – Sourav Ganguly, V V S Laxman, Virender Sehwag – began to reduce the burden on Sachin's shoulders, we earned his respect. That was important. For me it was important to know that I had earned the right to share the same dressing room with him. So what made him stand out even in a team of outstanding batsmen?

His cricketing nous is exceptional. He honed his skills by batting for so many hours as a youngster. Even today, after all the records and the adulation and the achievements, he loves to bat – in the nets, at the matches, against anybody, any time because he simply loves to bat on and on. I wouldn't be surprised if he batted in his drawing room with his children throwing the ball at him, or in the garage playing the ball rebounding from a wall.

Cricket is a team game with an individual flavour – the bowler at the top of his mark, the fielder waiting beneath a skier or the batsman awaiting the next delivery are all lonely men aware of this loneliness. Don Bradman hit golf balls against the water tank in his backyard in preparation for the lonely hours at the crease. Sachin was luckier – older players took him seriously enough to let him bat on. But before he got so organised, there was the compound wall and the domestic help who were pressed into service.

"Don't motivate him any further," I once heard of a bowler complaining, "for that will mean many more hours of bowling to him at the nets."

Sachin Tendulkar wins yet another Man of the Series award, Sir Gary Sobers does the honours.

For that is the other remarkable thing about Sachin. He needs no outsider to turn the keys of motivation. Everything he needs – motivation, inspiration, critical assessment, challenge, goal-setting, coaching, psychological boosts – he finds within himself. Such amazing self-sufficiency comes with an equally amazing self-awareness. It is a combination that is unique and has made him what he is. Part of this is conscious, sharpened by experience; but much of it comes naturally, without conscious thought. I know no player who has Sachin's ability to analyse his own game. He is a skilled analyst with a finely-honed instinct.

His mantra is simple: keep it simple. He knows exactly what works for him, is always aware of his precise state of mind, knows when his game is right, and above all, knows how to score runs even when all these factors are not in harmony. His solutions to specific problems are specific. No catch-all solutions for him. Over many years, batsmen work out what makes them tick. Call it experience, call it familiarity with the craft, call it what you will, but much time is wasted in the process going down blind alleys and mooring your craft to unsteady piers. Sachin, like a musical prodigy who hits the right note the day he picks up a violin, hit the right note the day he picked up a bat. The rest has been merely refinement.

It has been fascinating watching the changes in his approach. From being a blaster, he is now a mistake-proof batsman. He truly enjoys the game, as much at 37 as he did at 15, and he communicates this enjoyment to millions across the world. This is because of his remarkable mind with its rare cricket intelligence. Rather like Sherlock Holmes who claimed he didn't need to know whether the sun rose in the east or west because that didn't help him in his profession, Sachin shut out anything that might have distracted him in the early years. As he grew older, he relaxed more, enjoying both the game and what it had to offer, like the travel. This is in contrast to some modern cricketers who begin by enjoying the non-cricketing aspects, and then if they last long enough learn to tighten up more.

By the age of 16 he had hit
more cricket balls than I had at 25

Like most great batsmen, Sachin has the ability to control where the bowlers bowl to him. Sometimes he goes on all-out attack as he did against Shane Warne in Chennai in 1998. Sometimes not attacking is the key, as when he elaborately leaves deliveries outside the off stump, forcing the bowler to bowl straighter at him. This he loves because he can then play off his legs. The flick he plays behind square leg to the fast bowlers, often taking the ball right off his stumps, is uniquely his. It is all about perfection and balance.

Above all, he has the ability to adapt. In the West Indies in '97, against Curtly Ambrose, Courtney Walsh, Ian Bishop and Franklyn Rose on a tricky Trinidad pitch, Sachin sized up the situation quickly and unleashed a flurry of strokes to disconcert the bowlers. His 44 had ten boundaries. Whether he makes 20 or 200, a Sachin innings is fascinating, as much for what he does as for what he does not do. A good example of the latter is his double century in Sydney when he decided to eliminate the cover drive because he had been getting out while attempting it.

It has helped that cricket is the one thing he has known in life, as is inevitable when you make your international debut at 16. Cricket means everything to him. A recent sportsman like that would be Pete Sampras who was wedded to tennis. Sachin knows what works for him, and is loath to take on too much outside of the actual business of making runs and winning matches.

He has been a successful leader and in the larger context of the game, that is more important. I have no time for excessive theory in air conditioned classrooms where someone tells us what is right and wrong and how to conduct ourselves and then goes out and behaves in a manner contrary to his preaching. Rather than making speeches, Sachin remained Sachin, and youngsters learnt from watching, absorbing almost subconsciously his attitude and his work ethic. He is a great motivator because his own motivation levels are so high. He walks the walk, and seldom talks the talk for the sake of talking. I always admired that.

He came into Tests a finished product

We take it for granted now when India are expected to win every match and dominate every series abroad, but when Sachin started out, a good draw abroad with an occasional win was considered a great result. We drew every match of his first series in Pakistan, and that was considered a triumph.

For years while the rest of the batting matured, he carried the team single-handedly. And as the victories at home, and more importantly, abroad pile up, he – and the rest of us – will be making way for a generation which believes that winning is its birthright. The diffidence of old has made way for the confidence of youth. Talent is not held back by the baggage of ancient history but inspired by the heroics of recent history. And Sachin's role in charting that course has been phenomenal.

There is no rule that sportsmen have to be paragons of virtue, but Sachin's attitude to sport, his humility, his constant desire to improve influenced those of us who followed. It helped that India's finest batsman was an ornament to the game itself. The culture he created sustained a whole generation of players. But every generation has to reinforce that culture, and not take it for granted. I was lucky that when I first played for India, players like Sachin and Anil Kumble were setting the standards of conduct that made it all special and uniquely Indian.

Yet, for all his achievements Sachin has sometimes been treated harshly. This is partly because of the high standards he himself has set. Successful players tend to be judged more harshly than others. That, I suppose, is a backhanded compliment. It is a recognition that more is expected because the player has more to give. Of course, excessive criticism hurts and Sachin is human after

Mobiles

all (it is important to remember this!), but he also knows that as a public figure he will be critiqued for his performances even if unfairly at times. All sportsmen are prepared for this.

On his bad days, Sachin's worry is not what people will think if he fails, but how much it will hurt the team and his teammates. We have spent hours together, talking, discussing batsmanship and, as is inevitable when you spend so much time together in stress situations, have been both honest and unguarded with each other.

To me, it is incredible that someone who has been playing continuously for over two decades retains the essential innocence and vulnerability of childhood. Sachin is no Peter Pan, the child who never grew up; rather he somehow nurtured the child in him so that even after more Tests and more runs and more centuries than anyone else, he plays with the enthusiasm and competitiveness of a child whose whole world is encompassed by those 22 yards.

When we walked off the field after beating Australia in Bangalore, my home town in October 2010, we were both highly emotional. But we hardly spoke to each other. Each knew exactly what the other was thinking and there was no need for words. Sharing a dressing room with Sachin has been a privilege. Sharing an unspoken thought raises a relationship above the merely professional. In over a decade and a half there have been many such moments. I cherish them just as much as I cherish the runs we made together for the country.

RAHUL DRAVID is one of only six players to make over ten thousand runs in two forms of the game. Tendulkar has been his teammate in over 127 Tests, a world record.

adidas
SAHARA

SAHARA

GENIUSPEAK

If I could be half of what my father was
I'd be a very good person in life.

At least with me,
the match starts much
much earlier than the actual match.

Your thought process changes.
When you have a fit body, you think differently, but when
you're not 100 percent fit, then your mind works differently.
Thinking is everything in this game.

A couple of times I tried going out
for the evening in disguise but it didn't work too well.
Now when I go to pray I go late at night to temples
which are empty and quiet.

I got out to Hansie Cronje more than anyone ...
I never knew what to do with him.

I am very happy that it came at this moment.
Yesterday was my father's birthday, and
I dedicate this to him.
(on reaching his 50th Test century)

If only one man is representing India in cricket,
then yes, blame that person
when things go wrong.

I could say that I didn't get to do all
those things that a normal teenager would do,
but then again, not many people get the opportunity
to do what I do.

Change is part of our lives, and as you get older,
you try to reach your destination in safer ways.

When you start thinking about bad times,
they come sooner than expected.

I would liked to have asked Hobbs and Hutton
what it was like to play on
uncovered wickets.

I believe every time I go out to bat, the country needs me.
Even if I go in at 200 for two, my frame of mind is the same.
It's that hunger which keeps me going.

Somewhere there's still a 16-year-old
inside who wants to go out and express himself,
I also love going for a drive at about 5am,
when the roads are empty and people won't see me.

Hundred percent commitment
is not too much to expect is it?

When there is time to think about cricket,
I think, but when it is time to be with family,
I try to do justice to that aspect of my life as well.

I had been hit on the nose
in school cricket on bad practice wickets, an experience that
had got rid of the fear. So when I was hit by Waqar, that got me
more competitive and I decided not to move from the middle.

My father, who died in 1999, was never a cricket fan,
not at all. He was a writer and a poet: he taught Marathi,
my mother tongue, at the local university. But
he understood exactly how to get the best out of me.
He warned me against taking short cuts and told me
to just keep playing, despite the ups and downs.

Twenty20 cricket is the dessert and
you can't survive on that. Who wants to eat
only desserts?

Life without cricket is unthinkable for me.

If I was chasing records, I wouldn't have missed
so many one-day internationals
when my body wasn't in the best shape.

INTO THE STAT-O-SPHERE

Ananthanarayanan

SACHIN TENDULKAR: IN FIGURES – TEST MATCHES

To reduce Tendulkar to mere figures is sacrilege. How can mere numbers define the grace, economy of movement, twinkling footwork, the turn of the wrist at the last second, the straightest of bats when defending, the unwavering concentration et al. The numbers can never bring out the impeccable behaviour, whitest of white career slate and the role-model image for the youth of India. Just as numbers can never define the true greatness of Roger Federer, numbers can never do justice to Tendulkar's career. However numbers can embellish the great players' careers, enhance their aura and form the jewels on their crowns.

These figures are current upto the end of the third Test between South Africa and India which finished on 6 January 2011.

The numbers speak for themselves. So no special comments have been provided.

1. CAREER SUMMARY:

Batting

Mat	Ins	NO	Runs	Avg	100	50	Freq	HS
177	290	32	14692	56.95	51	59	5.7	248*

Fielding

Catches
106

Bowling

Overs	Runs	Wickets	Average	RpO	Best Bowling
682.4	2388	45	53.06	3.49	3 for 14

2. Runs by Innings:

Mat	Ins	NO	Runs	Avg	100	50	Freq
In-1	83	6	5397	70.09	20	19	4.2
In-2	91	3	5160	58.64	18	22	5.1
In-3	66	8	2764	47.66	10	13	6.6
In-4	50	15	1371	39.17	3	5	16.7

Celebrating with friends.

3. Summary by Batting position:

Mat	Ins	NO	Runs	Avg	100	50	Freq
2	1	0	15	15.00	0	0	1.0
4	237	26	12275	58.18	44	49	5.4
5	28	3	1540	61.60	5	6	5.6
6	20	3	745	43.82	2	4	10.0
7	4	0	117	29.25	0	0	4.0

4. Summary by Match location:

	Mat	Ins	NO	Runs	Avg	100	50	Freq
Home	79	130	15	6547	56.93	22	27	5.9
Away	98	160	17	8145	56.96	29	32	5.5

5. Results Summary:

	Mat	Ins	NO	Runs	Avg	100	50	Freq
Won	61	97	16	5473	67.57	20	21	4.8
Drawn	70	101	14	5788	66.53	20	25	5.0
Lost	46	92	2	3431	38.12	11	13	8.4

6. Peer comparisons:

	SRT	Others	Ratio
All players	56.95	37.10	153.5%
India players	56.95	40.31	141.3%

Indicates Tendulkar's high proportion of runs; the lower ratio indicates India's superior batting line-up.

7. Share of team batting:

Total team runs : 93480
Share : 15.72%

8. Average Batting Position: 4.27

Indicates that Tendulkar has batted at no.4 for over 80% of his innings.

9. Time spent on field:

Balls faced:	27123	Hours:	339.0
Other Batsmen faced:	25852	Hours:	287.2
Balls bowled:	4096	Hours:	45.5
Balls fielded:	169199	Hours:	1692.0
Total hours:	2363.8		
Avge hours per match:	13.35		

10. Summary by country:

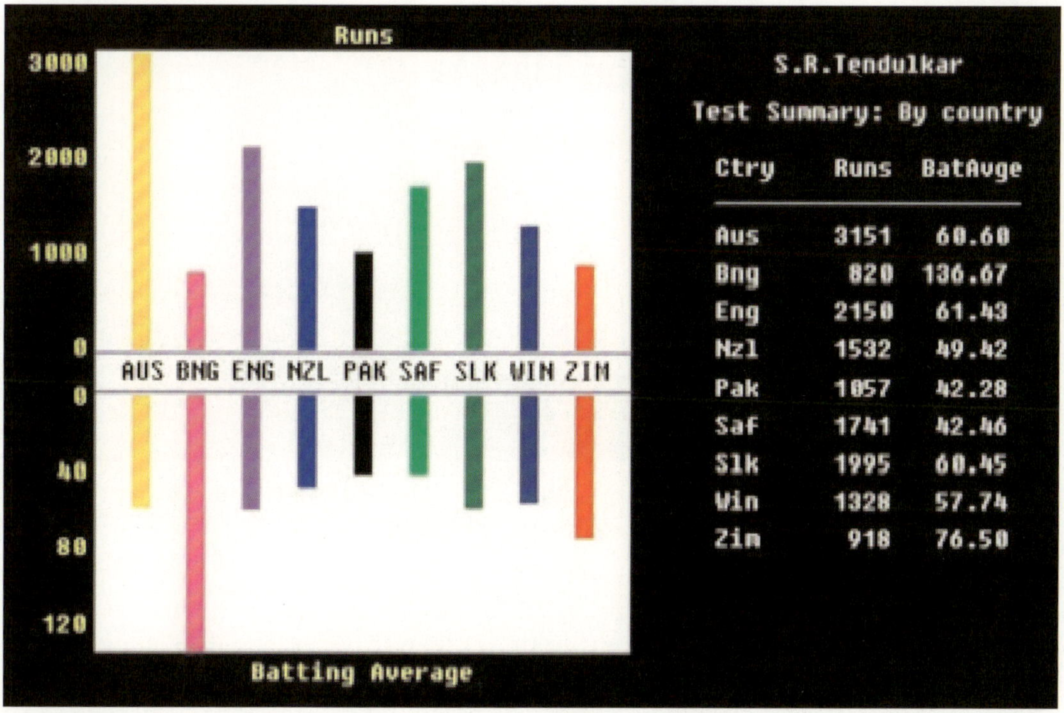

Country	Mat	Ins	NO	Runs	Avg	100	50	Freq
Australia	31	59	7	3151	60.60	11	13	5.4
Bangladesh	7	9	3	820	136.67	5	0	1.8
England	24	39	4	2150	61.43	7	10	5.6
New Zealand	22	36	5	1532	49.42	4	8	9.0
Pakistan	18	27	2	1057	42.28	2	7	13.5
South Africa	25	45	4	1741	42.46	7	5	6.4
Sri Lanka	25	36	3	1995	60.45	9	6	4.0
West Indies	16	25	2	1328	57.74	3	7	8.3
Zimbabwe	9	14	2	918	76.50	3	3	4.7

11. Summary by year:

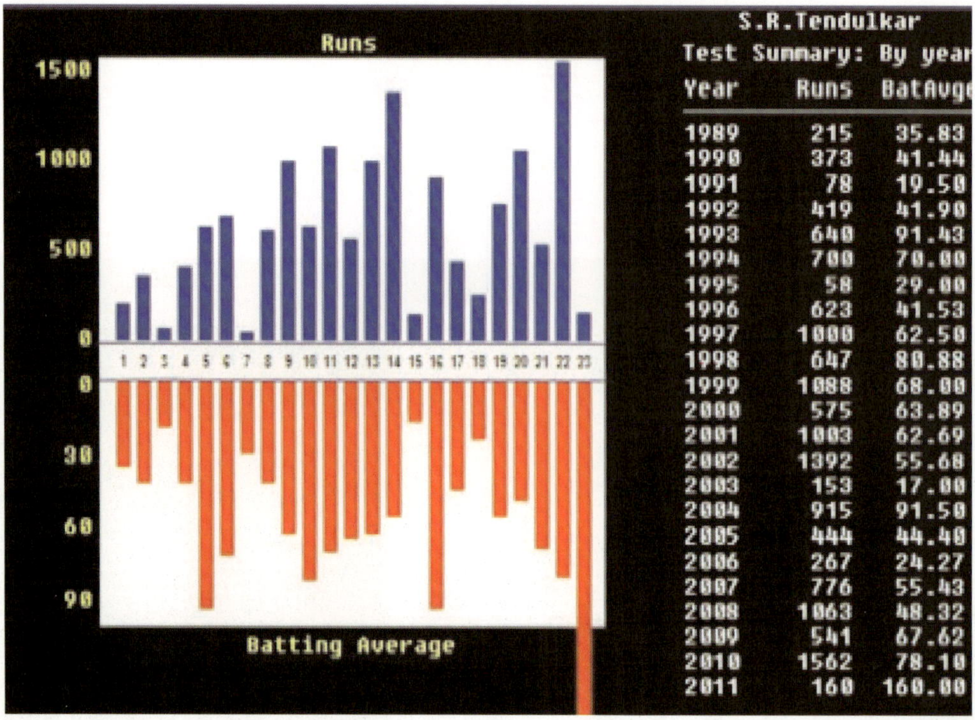

Year	Mat	Ins	NO	Runs	Avg	100	50	Freq
1989	4	6	0	215	35.83	0	2	6.0
1990	7	10	1	373	41.44	1	2	10.0
1991	2	4	0	78	19.50	0	0	4.0
1992	7	11	1	419	41.90	3	0	3.7
1993	8	9	2	640	91.43	2	5	4.5
1994	7	11	1	700	70.00	2	3	5.5
1995	3	4	2	58	29.00	0	1	4.0
1996	8	15	0	623	41.53	2	2	7.5
1997	12	17	1	1000	62.50	4	3	4.2
1998	5	9	1	647	80.88	3	1	3.0
1999	10	19	3	1088	68.00	5	4	3.8
2000	6	10	1	575	63.89	2	1	5.0
2001	10	18	2	1003	62.69	3	6	6.0
2002	16	26	1	1392	55.68	4	5	6.5
2003	5	9	0	153	17.00	0	1	9.0

2004	10	15	5	915	91.50	3	2	5.0
2005	6	10	0	444	44.40	1	3	10.0
2006	8	12	1	267	24.27	0	1	12.0
2007	9	16	2	776	55.43	2	6	8.0
2008	13	25	3	1063	48.32	4	3	6.2
2009	6	9	1	541	67.62	2	3	4.5
2010	14	23	3	1562	78.1	7	5	3.3
2011	1	2	1	160	160.00	1	0	2.0

12. Analysis of 10-match streaks:

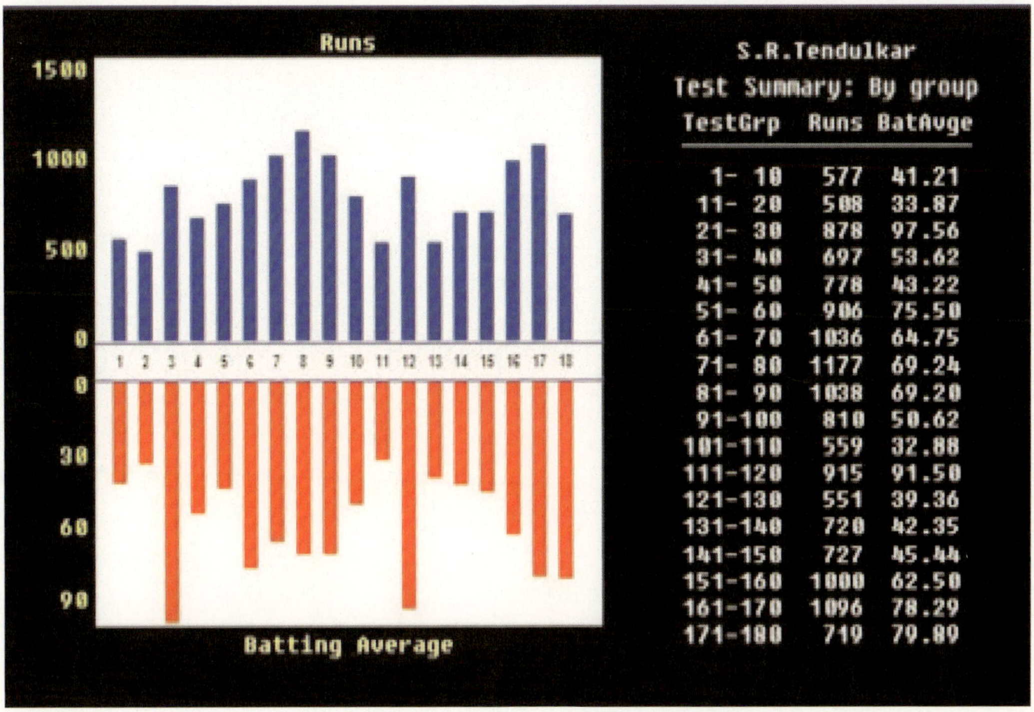

	Mat	Ins	NO	Runs	Avg
1 to 10	10	15	1	577	41.21
11 to 20	10	16	1	508	33.87
21 to 30	10	11	2	878	97.56
31 to 40	10	16	3	697	53.62
41 to 50	10	19	1	778	43.22
51 to 60	10	13	1	906	75.50

61 to 70	10	19	3	1036	64.75
71 to 80	10	18	1	1177	69.24
81 to 90	10	17	2	1038	69.20
91 to 100	10	16	0	810	50.62
101 to 110	10	18	1	559	32.88
111 to 120	10	15	5	915	91.50
121 to 130	10	15	1	551	39.36
131 to 140	10	18	1	720	42.35
141 to 150	10	18	2	727	45.44
151 to 160	10	19	3	1000	62.50
161 to 170	10	15	1	1096	78.29
171 to 180	7	12	3	719	79.89

12a. Best streak:

162-171	10	16	2	1323	94.50

12b. Worst streak:

126-135	10	16	1	387	25.80

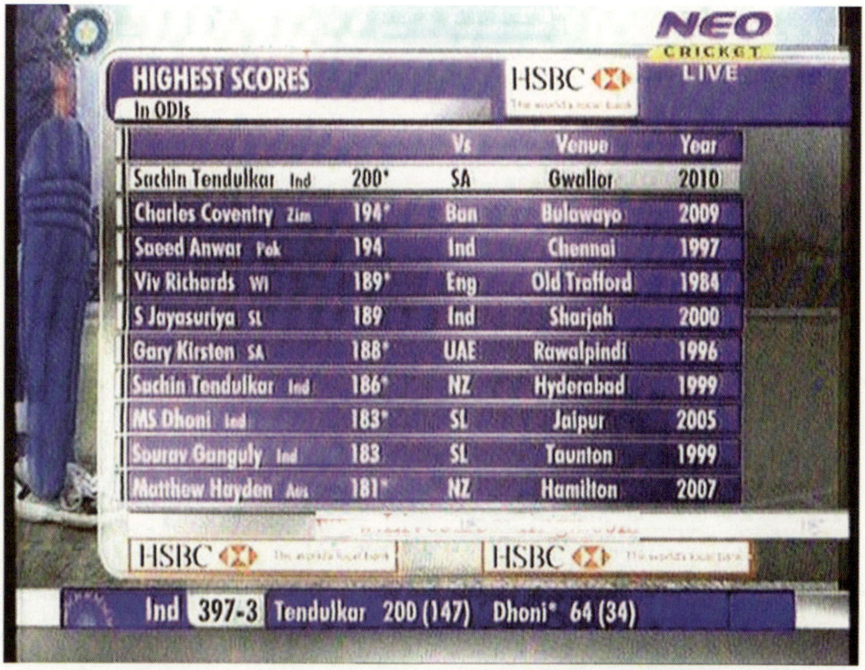
NEO CRICKET LIVE
HIGHEST SCORES
In ODIs
HSBC
Vs Venue Year
Sachin Tendulkar Ind 200* SA Gwalior 2010
Charles Coventry Zim 194* Ban Bulawayo 2009
Saeed Anwar Pak 194 Ind Chennai 1997
Viv Richards WI 189* Eng Old Trafford 1984
S Jayasuriya SL 189 Ind Sharjah 2000
Gary Kirsten SA 188* UAE Rawalpindi 1996
Sachin Tendulkar Ind 186* NZ Hyderabad 1999
MS Dhoni Ind 183* SL Jaipur 2005
Sourav Ganguly Ind 183 SL Taunton 1999
Matthew Hayden Aus 181* NZ Hamilton 2007
HSBC
HSBC
Ind 397-3 Tendulkar 200 (147) Dhoni* 64 (34)

The Indian EXPRESS
God!
SAHARA INDIA
SACHIN TENDULKAR 200*
First double century in the 39-year history of ODIs helps India beat South Africa by 153 runs, take series. Tendulkar now has 46 hundreds in ODIs, 47 in Tests.

SACHIN TENDULKAR: AN ANALYTICAL SUMMARY OF HIS ODI CAREER

The numbers speak for themselves. So no special comments have been provided.

1. Career Summary:

	Mat	Ins	NO	Runs	Avg	100	50	Freq	Balls	S/R	HS
Career	442	431	41	17598	45.12	46	93	9.4	20401	86.3	200*
Opening	319	319	23	14482	48.93	42	72	11.0	16431	88.1	200*

2. Runs by Innings:

	Mat	Ins	NO	Runs	Avg	100	50	Freq	Balls	S/R
Inns 1	213	212	15	9216	46.78	29	43	7.3	10935	84.3
Inns 2	229	219	26	8382	43.43	17	50	12.9	9470	88.5

3. Summary by match location:

	Mat	Ins	NO	Runs	Avg	100	50	Freq	Balls	S/R
Home	156	152	15	6522	47.61	18	36	8.4	7401	88.1
Neutral	146	140	16	6203	50.02	17	33	8.2	7072	87.1
Away	140	139	10	4873	37.78	11	24	12.6	5932	82.1

4. Results summary:

	Mat	Ins	NO	Runs	Avg	100	50	Freq	Balls	S/R
Won	222	219	34	10737	58.04	33	56	6.6	11846	90.6
Lost	193	193	2	6312	33.05	12	35	16.1	7928	79.6
No Res	27	19	5	549	39.21	1	2	19.0	631	87.0

5. Peer Comparisons with other batsmen:

Others' Batting average: 29.52 Ratio: 152.9%

Others' Strike rate: 79.6 Ratio: 108.4%

6. Share of team batting:

Total team Runs: 97211 Share: 18.1%

7. Avg Batting Position: 0.61 (opening position is 0)

8. Time spent on field:

Balls faced:	20401	Hours:	255.0
Other Batsmen faced:	21095	Hours:	234.4
Balls bowled:	8026	Hours:	89.2
Balls fielded:	109168	Hours:	1091.7
Total hours:	1670.3		
Avg hours per match:	3.78		

9. Summary by country:

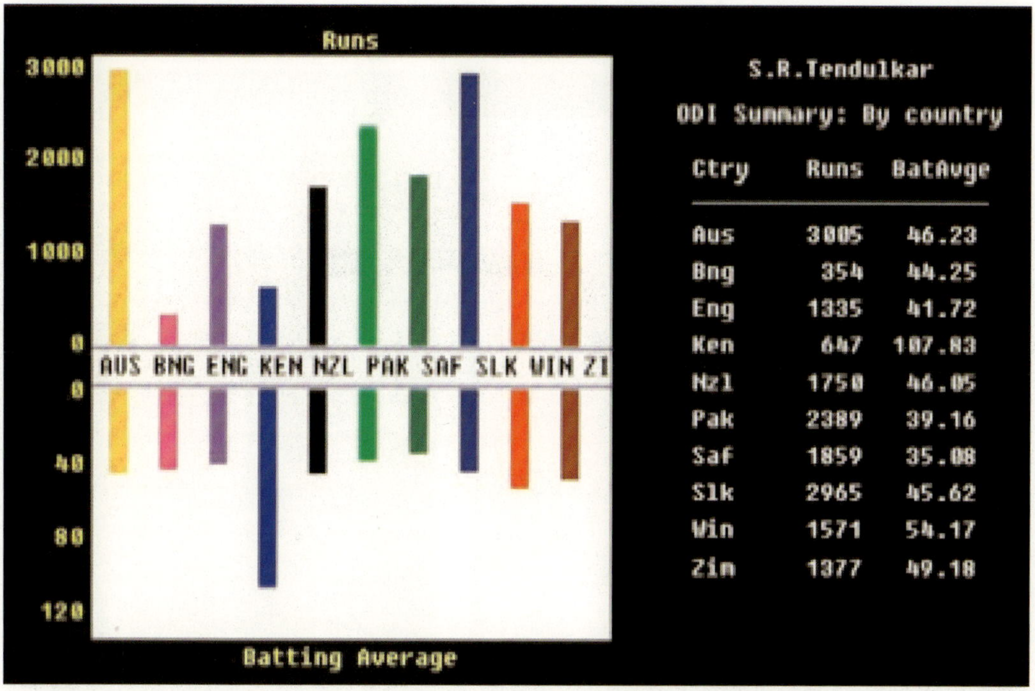

	Mat	Ins	NO	Runs	Avg	100	50	Freq	Balls	S/R
Aus	67	66	1	3005	46.23	9	14	7.3	3534	85.0
Bng	10	9	1	354	44.25	0	2	9.0	407	87.0
Eng	36	36	4	1335	41.72	1	10	36.0	1513	88.2
Ken	10	9	3	647	107.83	4	1	2.2	665	97.3
Hol	1	1	0	52	52.00	0	1	0.0	72	72.2
Nzl	42	41	3	1750	46.05	5	8	8.2	1836	95.3
Pak	67	65	4	2389	39.16	5	14	13.0	2724	87.7

Saf	54	54	1	1859	35.08	4	8	13.5	2463	75.5
Slk	78	74	9	2965	45.62	8	17	9.2	3385	87.6
UAE	2	2	0	81	40.50	0	1	2.0	102	79.4
Win	38	38	9	1571	54.17	4	11	9.5	2017	77.9
Zim	34	33	5	1377	49.18	5	5	6.6	1504	91.6
Ire	1	1	0	4	4.00	0	0	0.0	3	133.3
Nam	1	1	0	152	152.00	1	0	1.0	151	100.7
Ber	1	1	1	57	57.00	0	1	0.0	29	196.6

10. Summary by year:

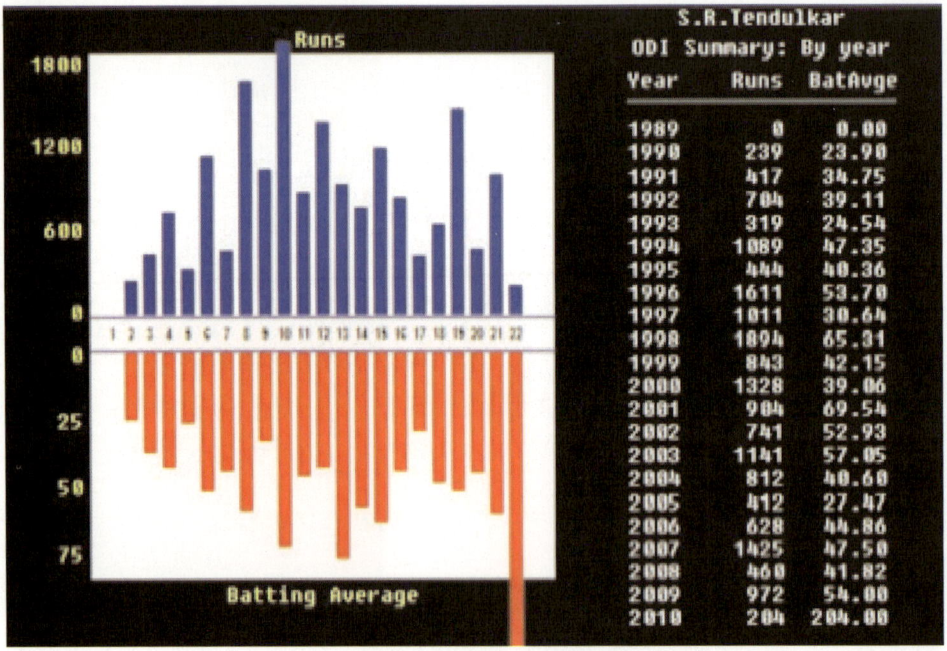

	Mat	Ins	NO	Runs	Avg	100	50	Freq	Balls	S/R
1989	1	1	0	0	0.00	0	0	0.0	2	0.0
1990	11	10	0	239	23.90	0	1	10.0	242	98.8
1991	14	14	2	417	34.75	0	4	14.0	560	74.5
1992	21	20	2	704	39.11	0	6	20.0	1016	69.3
1993	18	17	4	319	24.54	0	1	17.0	433	73.7
1994	25	25	2	1089	47.35	3	9	8.3	1236	88.1
1995	12	12	1	444	40.36	1	1	12.0	438	101.4
1996	32	32	2	1611	53.70	6	9	5.3	1956	82.4

1997	39	36	3	1011	30.64	2	5	18.0	1190	85.0
1998	34	33	4	1894	65.31	9	7	3.7	1854	102.2
1999	22	22	2	843	42.15	3	1	7.3	952	88.6
2000	34	34	0	1328	39.06	3	6	11.3	1624	81.8
2001	17	16	3	904	69.54	4	3	4.0	990	91.3
2002	20	19	5	741	52.93	2	3	9.5	847	87.5
2003	21	21	1	1141	57.05	3	8	7.0	1306	87.4
2004	21	21	1	812	40.60	1	5	21.0	1014	80.1
2005	16	16	1	412	27.47	1	2	16.0	533	77.3
2006	16	16	2	628	44.86	2	3	8.0	815	77.1
2007	33	32	2	1425	47.50	1	13	32.0	1665	85.6
2008	12	12	1	460	41.82	1	3	12.0	546	84.2
2009	21	20	2	972	54.00	3	3	6.7	1034	94.0
2010	2	2	1	204	204.00	1	0	2.0	152	134.2

11. Analysis by 20-match streaks:

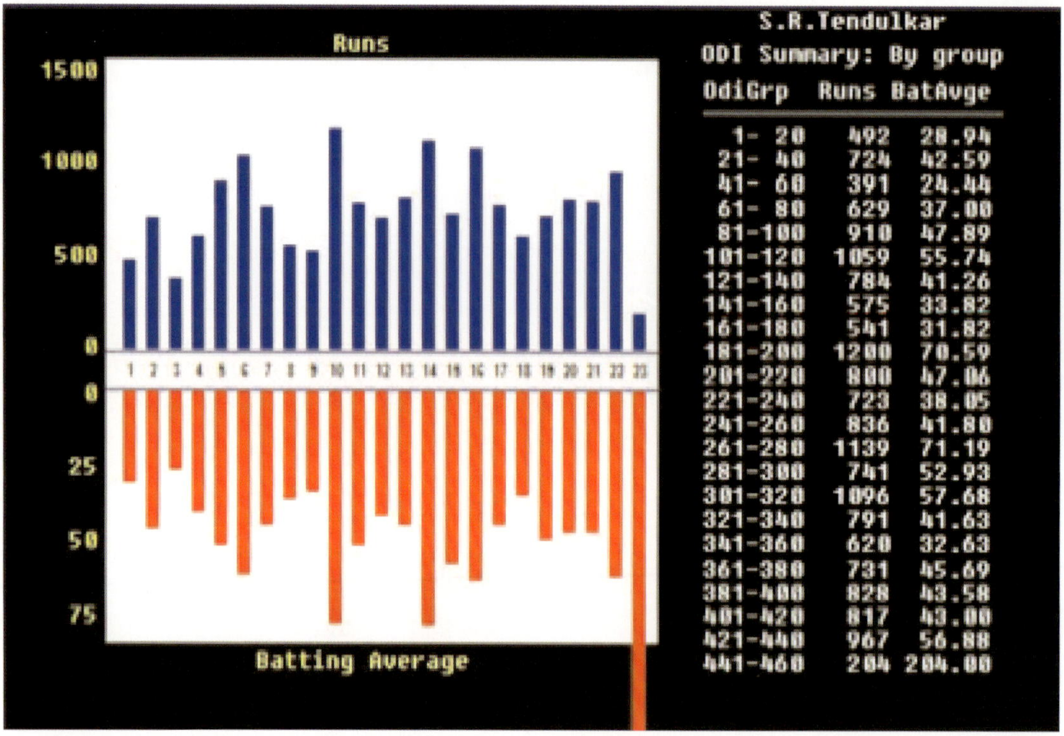

	Mat	Ins	NO	Runs	Avg	Balls	S/R
1-20	20	19	2	492	28.94	528	93.2
21-40	20	19	2	724	42.59	1035	70.0
41-60	20	19	3	391	24.44	567	69.0
61-80	20	20	3	629	37.00	707	89.0
81-100	20	20	1	910	47.89	1026	88.7
101-120	20	20	1	1059	55.74	1261	84.0
121-140	20	20	1	784	41.26	962	81.5
141-160	20	19	2	575	33.82	674	85.3
161-180	20	18	1	541	31.82	571	94.7
181-200	20	19	2	1200	70.59	1204	99.7
201-220	20	20	3	800	47.06	842	95.0

221-240	20	20	1	723	38.05	846	85.5
241-260	20	20	0	836	41.80	1003	83.3
261-280	20	19	3	1139	71.19	1267	89.9
281-300	20	19	5	741	52.93	847	87.5
301-320	20	20	1	1096	57.68	1240	88.4
321-340	20	20	1	791	41.63	1006	78.6
341-360	20	20	1	620	32.63	763	81.3
361-380	20	19	3	731	45.69	906	80.7
381-400	20	20	1	828	43.58	1056	78.4
401-420	20	20	1	817	43.00	924	88.4
421-440	20	19	2	967	56.88	1018	95.0
441-460	2	2	1	204	204.00	152	134.2

11a. Best streak:

185-204	20	19	3	1314	82.12	1308	100.5

11b. Worst streak:

49-68	20	19	4	301	20.07	438	68.7

12. Bowling Summary:

Overs: 1336.4
Runs: 6817
Wickets: 154
Average: 44.26
RPO: 5.10
Best Bowling: 5 for 32
Catches: 134

PEERSPEAK

*I'd like to see him go out one day and bat with a stump.
I tell you, he'd do OK.*

- Grey Chappell

He should aim for more. Maybe a Test innings of 450 or an ODI knock of 250. There is a little boy in Tendulkar who wants to keep playing. That spirit keeps him going.

- Sunil Gavaskar

You take Don Bradman away and he's next up, I reckon.

- Steve Waugh

*Jessie! Come here, look. The batsman on television.
Don't you think he reminds you of me?*

- Don Bradman

If I had a son I would have wanted him to play like Sachin.

- Brian Lara

He never comes late to any practice session, never comes late to the team bus, never comes late to any meeting - he is always five minutes ahead of time.

- Virender Sehwag

Every run that comes off Sachin's blade is a record. He has shown the world how to perform under pressure.

- Sharad Pawar

This little prick's going to overtake your record, AB.

- Merv Hughes to Allan Border

Better than Brian Lara and Ricky Ponting, the other two great players of my era. Better than Sir Viv Richards, Sunil Gavaskar and Allan Border. And I would even say better than Sir Don Bradman himself.

- Nasser Hussain

To me he will not just be remembered as a great player and a lovely human being, but as somebody who tried to learn Bengali for the last 14 years but never managed to do so!

- Sourav Ganguly

I thought the way he celebrated when he reached his 200 epitomised the man's persona. There was no running laps around the field, no aggressive gestures, nothing over-the-top. He did what he always does, raised both his arms, closed his eyes for a moment and quietly acknowledged that it had been done.

- Anil Kumble

He is No. 1 in my book - the best player I have ever had the privilege of bowling to. There's Steve Waugh and there's Brian Lara, but Tendulkar is a class above, consistently special.

- Allan Donald

You can only marvel at the completeness of his career.

- Kumara Sangakkara

I have seen GOD , he bats at no.4 for India in Tests.

- Mathew Hayden

He is a perfectly balanced batsman and knows perfectly well when to attack and when to play defensive cricket. He has developed the ability to treat bowlers all over the world with contempt and can destroy any attack with utmost ease.

- Greg Chappell

He is cool, has magnificent temperament, and is so mature you tend to forget his age. I can't think of any other example of a player who has so dominated the world before the age of 25.

- Tony Greig

Nothing bad can happen to us if we're on a plane in India with Sachin Tendulkar on it.

-Hashim Amla

Sachin was so focussed. He never looked like getting out. He was batting with single-minded devotion. It was truly remarkable. It was a lesson.

- Martina Navratilova

Tennis legend joins the Sachin Tendulkar fan club after watching him bat at Sydney.

We're blessed to still have such a great player playing this game.

- Michael Clarke

Sachin impressed me when he really worked through his tennis elbow – that is the true sign of a champion.

- Mathew Hayden

He has been in form longer than some of our guys have been alive.

- Daniel Vettori

In an over I can bowl six different balls. But then Sachin looks at me with a sort of gentle arrogance down the pitch as if to say 'Can you bowl me another one?'

- Adam Hollioake

The archives recall not one single incriminating incident, not one drunken escapade, not one reported affair, not one spat with a team-mate or reporter ... Is he human?

- Michael Atherton

If I have to bowl to Sachin, I'll bowl with my helmet on.

- Dennis Lillee

There are two kind of batsmen in the world.
One Sachin Tendulkar.
Two all the others.

- Andy Flower

I would go to bed having nightmares of Sachin dancing down the ground and hitting me for sixes.

- Shane Warne

Thank God I won't be playing when he is 25.

- Allan Border

He has achieved everything, there is nothing more to achieve.

- Javed Miandad

He has defied age time and again. The depth of his passion is incomparable.

- Javagal Srinath

With Tendulkar, it's like the elephant in the room that no one wants to talk about.

- Sanjay Manjrekar

on why Sachin's failures, especially while chasing, are not questioned by the media

He has defined cricket in his fabulous, impeccable manner. He is to batting what Shane Warne is to bowling.

- Richie Benaud

He's 99.5 percent perfect.

- Viv Richards

Sachin Tendulkar is, in my time, the best player without doubt - daylight second, Brian Lara third.

- Shane Warne

Whenever we talk about cricket, we will talk about Sachin.

- Curtly Ambrose

A moment with contemporaries: Brian Lara(top) and Javed Miandad.

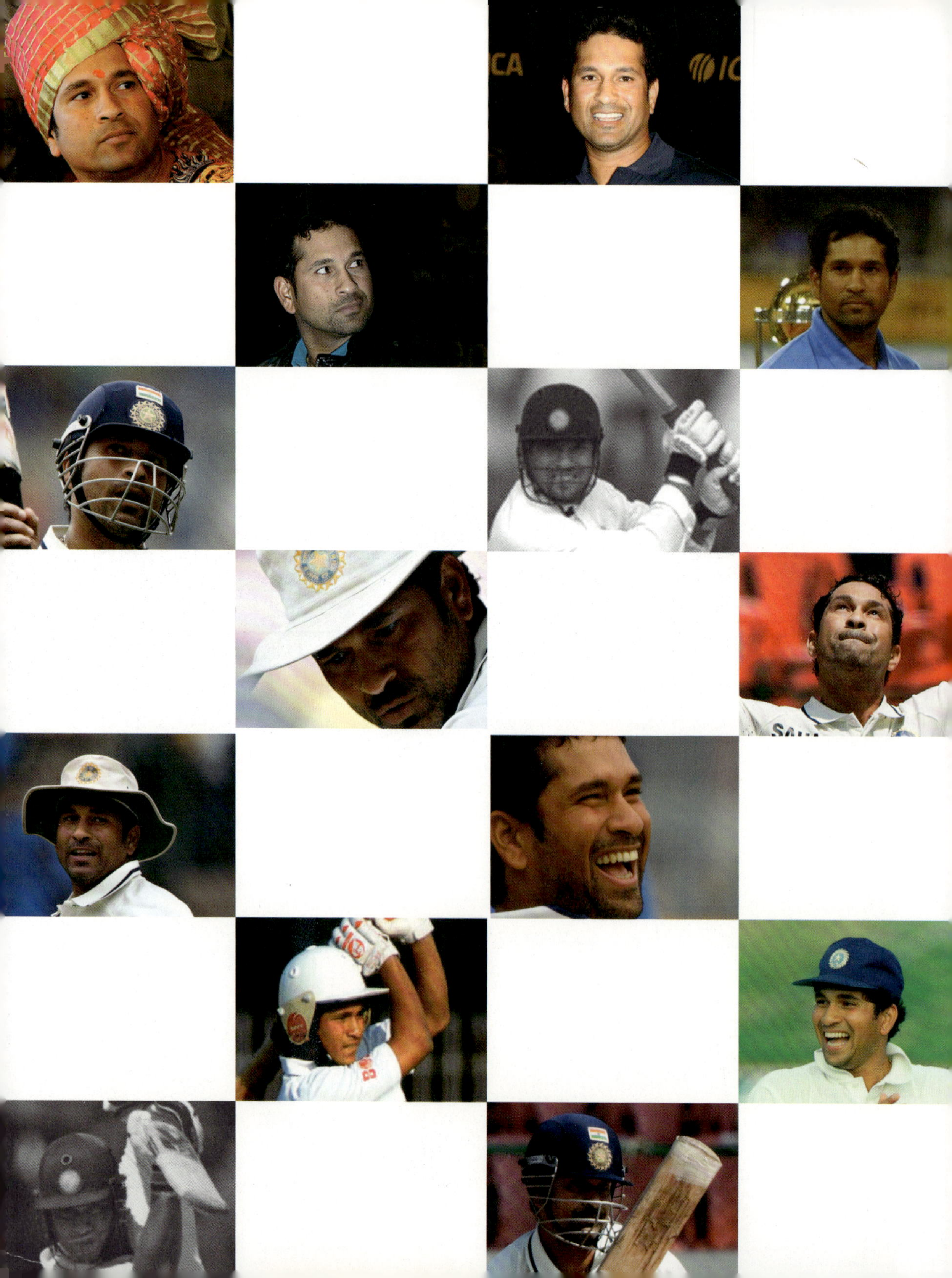